1 MINUTE TO RENTAL PROPERTY RICHES

"Learn To Make Money, Build Wealth, and Retire Early as a Landlord"

"The Truth, the Whole Truth, and Nothing but the Truth" about investing in rental properties including straight talk about finding rental properties at a huge discount; buying with no money down; how to calculate real world cash flow; nightmare tenants; evictions; how much work is really involved; tenant screening; dealing with bad tenants; the reasons newbies fail; and much more!

By

Michael Rossi

1 MINUTE TO RENTAL PROPERTY RICHES

Copyright©2006 Ciara International, Inc.

ISBN 978-1-4303-0806-5

Limits of Liability/Disclaimer of Warranty

All rights reserved. No part of this publication may be reproduced, distributed, or transmitted in any form or by any means, electronic or mechanical, including photocopying, recording, or any information storage and retrieval system now known or to be invented, without the prior written permission from the publisher, except by a reviewer who wishes to quote brief passages in connection with a review written for inclusion in a magazine, newspaper, or broadcast.

This publication was written with the intention to provide accurate information regarding the subject matter covered. It is sold with the understanding that neither the author nor the publisher is engaged in rendering investment advice, accounting advice, legal services, or any other professional services. If investment advice, accounting advice, legal services, or any other professional services are required, then the assistance of an appropriate professional should be sought.

Neither the author nor the publisher make any representation or warranty as to the completeness, accuracy, applicability, or fitness of any information presented in this publication. The author and the publisher disclaim any warranties (implied or expressed) and shall not be held responsible for any omissions, errors, or damages arising out of the use of this information. The reader is completely and solely responsible for any profit or loss resulting from his/her use of the information in this publication.

Investing in real estate involves risk. It is possible to do everything right and still lose money. No-one can guarantee that any individual or group will make money. These factors should be carefully considered before investing or beginning any new business.

This publication contains material protected by International and Federal Laws and Treaties.

About the Author

Michael Rossi

Michael is a real live investor in rental properties - NOT a professional seminar speaker, course provider, mentor, or real estate coach.

Mike has been successfully free from the 9-5 JOB scene for over 15 years. He has operated several successful businesses during that time.

Three years ago, Mike decided to transition his business to the "passive" income world of rental properties. Mike quickly discovered that the world of "passive" income from rental properties was not nearly as passive as the gurus would have you believe, and that the "guru" wisdom on real estate investing was simply...

WRONG!

Mike has discovered the truth about the real world of being a landlord and shares those truths with you in this book. These truths can make the difference between running a successful rental property business and being one of the vast majority of real estate newbies to fail.

The real world of real estate investing requires work and it takes time. That's why this book is entitled "1 Minute to Rental Property Riches". It is a sarcasm of the many real estate gurus that promise instant riches without work!

If you are looking for a motivational book that makes silly promises about instant riches without work, then you've got the wrong book!

If you are looking for a book that tells you the TRUTH about getting rich with rental properties, then this is the book you have been looking for!

This book covers everything you need to know about starting a rental property business, from writing a business plan to advanced landlording techniques. So if you are ready to start on the road to financial freedom with rental properties, get out your highlighter and prepare to start learning.

1 MINUTE TO RENTAL PROPERTY RICHES

How You Can Make Money, Build Wealth, and Retire Early as a Landlord

Table of Contents

Foreword…..Page 8

Making Money with Rental Properties…..Page 9
    Equity At Closing…..Page 9
    Cash Flow…..Page 9
    Pay Down of Principal…..Page 10
    Appreciation…..Page 10
    Tax Depreciation…..Page 10

Guru Nonsense! …..Page 12
    "The Secret"…..Page 12
    The No-Money, No Credit Myth…..Page 12
    Expenses…..Page 14
    Autopilot…..Page 15
    Be the Dealmaker Myth…..Page 16

Personality Test…..Page 17

Business Plan…..Page 20
    Rich…..Page 20
    Business Plan Basics…..Page 21
    Business Plan…..Page 22

Buying Right…..Page 27
    Education…..Page 27
    Real Estate Investors Association (REIA)…..Page 28
    Internet…..Page 28
    Learning Your Market…..Page 29
    Market Trends - Nationally and Locally…..Page 30
    Houses vs. Apartments…..Page 30
    Buying at a Discount - The 70% Rule…..Page 31

CASH FLOW…..Page 32
    Do It Yourself to EARN Extra Cash Flow…..Page 38
    The 2% Rule…..Page 39
    Summary of Rental Property Purchase Rules…..Page 39

1 MINUTE TO RENTAL PROPERTY RICHES

Locating Rental Properties…..Page 40
    Real Estate Agents…..Page 40
    REOs (Real Estate Owned by the Bank)…..Page 41
    Newspaper…..Page 42
    Drive Your Target Area…..Page 43
    Place an Ad of Your Own…..Page 44
    REIA (Real Estate Investors Association)…..Page 44
    Auctions…..Page 45
    Foreclosures and Sheriff Sales…..Page 45

Entity Structuring…..Page 46

Purchasing Techniques…..Page 47
    Pay Cash and Refinance…..Page 47
    Borrow the Money…..Page 48
    Other People's Money (OPM) or Credit (OPC)…..Page 50
    Owner Financing…..Page 50
    Subject to the Existing Financing (Sub to or Sub 2)…..Page 51
    Lease Options…..Page 52
    Selling with a Lease Option…..Page 53
    The Reality of Selling with a Lease Option…..Page 54
    Sandwich Lease Option…..Page 56
    Purchase Procedure…..Page 57

Rehabbing Rentals…..Page 59

Landlording Basics…..Page 62
    Finding Tenants…..Page 62
    Newspaper Ads…..Page 62
    Yard Sign…..Page 63
    Internet Sites…..Page 63
    Word of Mouth…..Page 63
    Other Tenants…..Page 63
    Section 8…..Page 63
    Screening Tenants…..Page 64
    Phone Screening…..Page 64
    Pet Policy…..Page 65
    The Second Call…..Page 67
    The Showing…..Page 67
    Visual Screening…..Page 68
    Taking the Application (and their application fee)…..Page 69

1 MINUTE TO RENTAL PROPERTY RICHES

Landlording Basics (con't)
    Criminal Background Check…..Page 69
    Credit Check…..Page 70
    Employment Check…..Page 70
    Previous Landlord Check…..Page 71
    Be the Manager, Not the Owner…..Page 72
    Privacy…..Page 74
    Prior to Move-In…..Page 75
    Lease…..Page 75
    Co-signer Form…..Page 76
    Pet Addendum…..Page 77
    Property Modification Agreement…..Page 77
    Paint Addendum…..Page 78
    Move-In/Move-Out Form…..Page 78
    Emergency Notification Form…..Page 78
    Lead Paint Disclosure Form and Lead Paint Pamphlet…..Page 79
    Utilities Transferred to Tenant's Name…..Page 79
    Keys…..Page 79
    Collecting the Rent…..Page 80
    Collecting Personally…..Page 80
    Collecting Remotely…..Page 80
    Late Fees…..Page 81
    Partial Rent…..Page 81
    Evictions…..Page 82
    Eviction for Non-Payment of Rent…..Page 83
    Evicting for Lease Violations …..Page 83
    Trick of the Trade…..Page 85
    Pay to Leave…..Page 85
    Do Not Discriminate…..Page 87

Landlording Nightmares - The True Story…..Page 88
    Crazy Daisy…..Page 88
    Chemical Attack…..Page 93
    No Good Deed Goes Unpunished…..Page 94
    Fire! …..Page 98
    The Nurse…..Page 99
    Dog…..Page 101
    Inheritance…..Page 103
    Priorities…..Page 106
    Tree Trouble…..Page 107
    Two for the Money…..Page 109

1 MINUTE TO RENTAL PROPERTY RICHES

Speaking Tenantese…..Page 114

Apartment Buildings and Complexes…..Page 117
      Why Invest in Apartment Buildings and Complexes?…..Page 117
      Special Considerations with Apartment Buildings and Complexes…..Page 118
      Money Talks…..Page 119
      Special Terminology…..Page 120
      Realistic Purchase Considerations…..Page 122
      Purchase Criteria…..Page 122

Now What? …..Page 123

Appendix…..Page 127
      Goals Worksheet…..Page 128
      Action Checklist…..Page 129
      Cash Flow Sheet…..Page 130
      Calculating Maximum Purchase Price…..Page 131
      Property Purchase Checklist…..Page 132
      Real Estate Purchase Contract…..Page 133
      Tenant Screening Policy…..Page 135
      Real Estate Leasing Checklist…..Page 136
      Deposit to Reserve Rental Unit…..Page 137
      Rental Application…..Page 138
      Residential Lease…..Page 139
      Residential Lease Addendum to Include Co-Signer…..Page 143
      Lease Addendum (General)…..Page 144
      Lease Addendum Allowing Pets…..Page 145
      Lease Addendum - Property Modification Agreement…..Page 146
      Lease Addendum - Paint Agreement…..Page 147
      Move-In/Move-Out Form…..Page 148
      Emergency Notification Form…..Page 150
      Lead Paint Disclosure Form…..Page 151
      Rent Receipt…..Page 152
      Rent Roll…..Page 153
      "For Rent" Flyer…..Page 154
      Newspaper Classified Ad…..Page 155
      Funding Request Cover…..Page 156
      Lead Paint Pamphlet…..Page 158

FOREWORD

Close your eyes for a moment. Think of where you will be five years from now. Will you still be working at the same dead-end 9 to 5 job? Is that your Dream? If you're like most people, the answer is a resounding NO! So, let's try that again. Where would you like to be 5 years from now? Would you like to be sitting on your yacht, sipping a tall drink with the beautiful people? Or maybe you would like to be flying on your personal jet to Europe for a month long vacation. Do you dream big? If so, maybe you'd like to be taking a year off and sailing around the world on your new 100-foot sailboat! Sounds great, doesn't it? **WAKE UP! THAT IS NOT GOING TO HAPPEN!**

This book is not about some silly fantasy. This book is about the REALITY of making money with rental properties. Can you get rich operating rental properties? YES! That's the good news. The bad news is that it will take a LOT of work and several years of your time. It will take sacrifice and a lot of determination. It will take some education. It will take some money or credit. If you are broke and your credit is ruined; if you are lazy and don't like to work; if you are looking for a get rich quick scheme; then being a landlord is probably not for you. Any thought to the contrary is simply nonsense.

This book is being written to fill a BIG void in the Real Estate Investing world. That void is REALITY! Most of today's real estate investing gurus make their money selling expensive courses, seminars, coaching, and mentoring. To draw in new customers, they paint an <u>extremely</u> optimistic view of real estate investing, particularly operating rental properties. This optimism comes in several forms. They underestimate the work involved. They underestimate the expenses involved. They underestimate the need for money or credit. They overestimate the money to be made.

These are great tactics for the gurus, whose objective is to draw in "newbies" and separate them from their money. However, it can be a disaster for the new investor who actually believes the hype.

In this book, I will tell you the truth as I know it. It won't be sugar coated and there won't be any hype. I won't be politically correct and some people may even be offended by the truth. Starting a rental business, or any business is difficult. The vast majority of people who try to start a business will fail in a very short period of time. If you are to have any chance of succeeding, you need to have the facts -- NOT A BUNCH OF MOTIVATIONAL NONSENSE! All the motivation in the world won't keep you in business if you don't have the cash flow!

If you've made it this far and are still thinking of getting started with real estate investing, then read on. I'll do my best to give you a look at the real world of being a landlord.

MAKING MONEY WITH RENTAL PROPERTIES

The phone began to ring. It was a call from my Realtor. A new REO had just come on the market and she thought I would be interested. A REO is Real Estate Owned by the bank, meaning a property that has been taken over by the bank following a foreclosure. I suggested that we meet at the house in an hour to take a look.

The house was a relatively small 2 bedroom, 1 bath house on a lower-middle income street. The paint was terrible (both inside and out); the carpet looked like it was purchased in the 1950s; and there were several holes in the walls. The asking price was only $19,000! I immediately made a written offer of $17,500 (cash) for the house. The bank quickly accepted and I bought the property. I put about $2,500 into rehabbing the property including new carpet, fixing the holes in the walls, and painting the entire house inside and out. I did all the work myself. All in all, it took about two weeks. Since that time, I have had the house rented for $500 per month. I refinanced the property along with some others to get my cash back. It appraised for $50,000.

This is a typical deal for me on a rental property. Let's see how many ways I made money on this deal:

1. **Equity at closing!**

   One of the first rules of purchasing rental properties is that you MUST buy at a discount. It is virtually impossible to buy a property at retail and then rent it out for a profit. In this case, I have $20,000 (purchase price + rehab) in this property and it is appraised at $50,000. Therefore, I picked up $30,000 in equity when I purchased this deal.

2. **Cash flow**

   Although this property was refinanced with some other properties, let's assume that it was refinanced alone. Financing $20,000 for 20 years at 7% results in a mortgage payment of $149 per month. Operating expenses (including paid management and maintenance) typically run 50% of gross rents, or $250 per month in this case. That leaves $250 to pay the mortgage. After the $149 mortgage is paid, I have a $101 profit each and every month. In other words, buying this property gave me an extra $101 per month or $1,212 per year of income! In reality, I actually make more than this because I manage this property and do the maintenance myself. Doing these jobs saves (makes) me about another $100 per month in income. Therefore, my real income from this property is $201 per month or $2,412 per year.

1 MINUTE TO RENTAL PROPERTY RICHES

3. **Pay Down of Principal**

    One of the exciting things about rentals is that the tenant pays the mortgage payment and all expenses for you. In this case, $149 of the $500 rent payment that I receive from the tenant goes to pay the mortgage. Obviously, part of that $149 pays the interest and part pays the principal. Over the 20 year term of the loan, the mortgage will be paid off and I'll own the house free and clear! So, with this rental property, the tenant is also paying me that $20,000 principal balance over 20 years, averaging $1,000 per year. Of course, in reality, the principle pay down starts out small and increases over the term of the loan.

4. **Appreciation**

    Historically, houses appreciate at 3% to 5% per year. Obviously, you shouldn't count on appreciation. Think of it as the icing on the cake.

    Let's consider the house I bought above. You will recall that it was worth $50,000. Even if it only appreciates 3% per year, that is another $1,500 in equity that I pick up each year! You'll note that I didn't have to do anything to get this equity. All I had to do was continue to own the property.

5. **Tax Depreciation**

    As if the previous four ways of making money weren't enough, the government has seen fit to allow you to depreciate your property. This can be a significant savings on your taxes and is the same as receiving additional money from your rental property. As of the writing of this book, properties are depreciated over a 27 1/2 year period. In the case of my little house, my yearly depreciation is $600. Remember, we can only depreciate the house (not the land) and only what we paid for the property, not the appraised value.

Are you getting excited yet? Let's add up the 1st year return that we're getting from one little $20,000 house.

1. Equity at closing	$30,000
2. Cash flow	$ 1,212
2A. Extra cash flow from doing management and maintenance myself	$ 1,200
3. Pay down of Principal (average)	$ 1,000
4. Appreciation	$ 1,500
5. Tax Depreciation	$ 600
Income and Equity at the End of Year One	**$35,512**

That's right! I essentially made $35,512 from a $20,000 investment in only one year!

Not Bad for a $20,000 Investment!

Now, consider for a moment that I don't have ANY of my own money in this deal. True, I did initially pay cash for this house, but I subsequently refinanced the property and got all of my money back! Of course, I could just as easily have borrowed the money from the bank to start with.

Moreover, after the first year I'll get an additional $5,512 in cash and equity each and every year (everything but the initial equity at closing).

Obviously, no-one is claiming to be rich on the basis of one deal like this. After all, even with performing all the management and maintenance myself, I'm only getting $2,412 cash per year, and I suspect that neither you or I could survive long on that! The equity that I picked up is helping to build wealth for the future.

You should now understand why operating rentals is such a powerful way to get rich! There are at least 5 ways that we can make money with rentals. Moreover, all of this can be accomplished without using any of our own money. Virtually no other form of investing allows the investor to make so much money without investing their own money.

To become rich, you simply need to decide how much money you want to make and then divide that by your cash flow per property. In our example, if you wanted to make $100,000 per year, then you would divide $100,000 by $2,412 to get 41. So, you would need 41 rentals at $2,412 cash flow per year to have an income of $100,000 per year. It really is just that simple.

GURU NONSENSE

One of your first stops on the road to success must be education. Therefore, I have included this chapter early in the book to give you my frank opinion on much of the material being presented by the popular real estate "gurus". Almost without exception, the various gurus have some good basic information to present. They are particularly good at teaching techniques to acquire property such as: subject-to, foreclosures, short sales, lease-options, etc. They are also good at teaching entity structuring and asset protection. Again, I'm not against spending money on education, but I do want to warn you about some of the popular guru ploys to get new investors to part with large chunks of their money. I also want to discuss some of the things that the gurus are particularly bad at teaching, like real world expenses and real world profits.

"The Secret"

Typically, the gurus reach a new investor through a free seminar or presentation. They present some basic information and then attempt to sell the "student" a course or seminar, usually costing between several hundred dollars and several thousand dollars. Most of the information in these courses is valid and can be used to make money with rental properties or whatever area of real estate investing that you are interested in. The problem with these guru systems is that they almost always present an unrealistically optimistic view of their particular technique. More disturbing is that almost all these gurus upsell the student into another more expensive course or seminar. During this upselling, the guru promises that the "secret" to success in real estate will be given in the next course. This cycle repeats at each level of training and the "secret" is never revealed. I want to make this point perfectly clear - **THERE IS NO SECRET!** Real estate investing is a very simple business whose principles are well established. There is NO secret to real estate and I don't pretend to give you one in this book.

The No-Money, No Credit Myth

WARNING: you are about to encounter some politically incorrect straight talk. Please realize that I am not trying to offend anyone. What I am trying to do is to give you realistic expectations regarding real estate investing in general, and rental properties in particular. In my opinion, it is unconscionable for anyone to give an unrealistically optimistic view of this business in order to get new investors to buy courses, seminars, coaching, or mentoring.

1 MINUTE TO RENTAL PROPERTY RICHES

A large part of the customer base for the real estate gurus is people who are down and out. These people often have no money, a lot of debt, and very little credit. The gurus imply through their infomercials and free seminars that these down-and-outers can somehow become rapidly rich. The infomercials almost always show the guru standing on a yacht; sitting by the pool at their mansion; or getting into their private jet. The TRUTH is that someone with no money and bad credit has a better chance of hitting the mega lotto than becoming rich in real estate. Please note that I'm not saying that you need a fortune in cash or a mountain of credit to start, but you do need something. I'm also not saying that someone with no money, a lot of debt, and very little credit can't become rich, but it will be VERY difficult.

The unpopular truth in today's politically correct world is that people are a product of their choices. If you are broke; have a lot of debt; and have very little credit, in most cases it is YOUR fault. YOU made bad choices.

If you have a bad job, in most cases it is your fault. If you are stuck on welfare, in most cases it is your fault. Whatever the problem, you must take personal responsibility for your situation.

You are not a VICTIM. An astounding percentage of our population goes through life thinking that they are a VICTIM. They blame their situation on someone or something else. This mentality will not take you far in the world of business and make no mistake… Operating Rental Properties IS a Business!

Another common malady in today's society is LAZINESS! By my calculation, at least 25% of the American population is simply Lazy. They don't work. They expect to be supported by the government. They think society owes them something!

What do all these people have in common?

1. They will never succeed without an attitude adjustment!

2. They live in rentals! (as landlords, they are our tenants)

Take an honest look in the mirror. Have I described you? If so, you must make some serious changes if you want to succeed in real estate investing, or anything else. You MUST take responsibility for your actions! You MUST make good choices! You are NOT a victim! No-one owes you anything! You MUST develop a work ethic!

Now that we've covered this tough topic, let's talk about what you CAN expect.

1 MINUTE TO RENTAL PROPERTY RICHES

Is it possible to BUY real estate with no money and no credit? Yes, it is. Only a small percentage of the possible deals are no money and no credit deals, but these deals can be found. I've personally done a lot of them. The problem with having no money and no credit is not that it's impossible to buy a property. The problem is that without a reserve of either money or credit, it is nearly impossible to run ANY business. Without a reserve, absolutely nothing can go wrong. Unfortunately, that is just not reality.

If you have no money and no credit, then do something about it. Take on a second or third job. Do whatever is necessary to save up some money and work on your credit BEFORE YOU START INVESTING IN REAL ESTATE.

Expenses

As I mentioned earlier, most of the gurus are notorious for being overly-optimistic. A big part of that, especially when it comes to rentals, is underestimating the expenses involved in the rental business. I have literally heard dozens of gurus speak and I have not heard one single guru properly discuss the expenses involved with rentals. In fact, I haven't heard even one guru that came close! I will be discussing exactly how to estimate rental expenses later in this book. However, for now let's look at an example of how the typical guru explains the operating expenses for rental properties. Before we do that let's define exactly what operating expenses are. Basically, operating expenses are all those expenses that are incurred by the landlord with the exception of the mortgage payment (principal and interest).

Here are the typical expenses listed in most guru courses:

1. Taxes
2. Insurance
3. Management
4. Maintenance
5. Vacancies

In fact, often the gurus don't even mention these expenses. I've read materials by supposed gurus that say the difference between the rent and the mortgage payment is your cash flow. These gurus have completely ignored ALL the operating expenses. That is absolute NONSENSE!

1 MINUTE TO RENTAL PROPERTY RICHES

Here are some of the REAL WORLD expenses that you will experience as a landlord:

1. Taxes
2. Insurance
3. Management
4. Maintenance
5. Vacancies
6. Evictions
7. Legal fees
8. Court costs
9. Entity maintenance
10. Damage caused by angry tenants
11. Office expenses/office supplies
12. Fuel for driving to and from your properties
13. Lawsuits
14. Capital expenses (new roof, furnace, etc)
15. Registration fees
16. Pest exterminations
17. Advertising
18. Many, many more!

You see that while most of the gurus only cover a few of the expenses, in the real world there are a BUNCH of additional expenses. Failing to prepare for these expenses will almost certainly result in a failed business. Therefore, it is imperative that you learn what these expenses are and how to evaluate a property based on the actual expenses! This topic is covered later in this book.

Autopilot

If I had a dollar for every guru course that promised new investors that they could run their real estate investing business on autopilot -- I'd be rich! Our society has gotten so fixated on doing everything fast and without work, that it has gotten to the point of being completely ridiculous! People buy all kinds of silly exercise machines on the promise that they can lose weight by exercising only a few minutes per day. The same is true of gurus promising their gullible students that they can get rich without much work. Somehow, everything is supposed to happen automatically. All you have to do is collect the piles of money as they roll in! RIDICULOUS!

Be the Dealmaker Myth

Another guru myth that is closely related to the Autopilot myth is the "Be the Dealmaker" myth. In this scenario, the new investor should spend his time looking for deals while hiring workers or contractors to do everything else. If this were not so laughable, it would be truly sad. The very last thing that a new investor should do is to waste money paying someone to do things he could do himself. Starting a successful business requires work, A LOT OF WORK! If you are not willing to work 10 to 12 hour days for the first year or two, then don't plan on leaving your day job. Even after your business is established, don't plan on spending all your time on your yacht. Successful people are typically workaholics. Think about Donald Trump. How many hours per day do you think he works? I'll bet that he works a lot more hours than you or I do. He deserves to be rich. He's worked hard for it!

With rental properties, it is especially important that you do the management and maintenance yourself. Typically, hiring a management company will cost you 10% of the gross rent. In many cases, this 10% of the gross rent will be a big part of your profit. Add another 5% to 10% of gross rents for paid maintenance and you can see that your entire profit can disappear if you hire these tasks out. Especially in the beginning, you should plan on doing as much work as you can. When your company grows to the point that you can no longer do everything, then you might think about hiring some help.

PERSONALITY TEST

Not everyone is cut out to be a professional football player. Very few people would argue with that. The same is true of being self-employed and of being a landlord. Here are some self-evaluation questions to help you decide if you are cut out to be a landlord:

1. Are you a self-starter? Without a boss to tell you what time to be at work, do you have the discipline to get up and go to work every day?

    Be honest! The majority of the people in the United States are NOT self-starters. They are more comfortable working in a structured environment where the hours are set and it is clearly known what is expected of them. Unfortunately, if you are not a self-starter, you won't make it in the rental property business.

2.. Are you able to make quick decisions and stick with them?

    This trait is certainly required of anyone that is self-employed. However, many people are just not wired this way. If you like to thoroughly analyze things at length before acting, then being self-employed is probably not for you.

3. Are you willing to work long hours for the next several years in order to reap big benefits in the future?

    Building a successful business will require sacrifice for the first several years. If you're not willing to work six 12-hour days each week for a couple of years, then you should not consider self-employment. Contrary to the guru hype, no one works harder than a new business owner.

4. Can you deal with chaos and still sleep at night?

    Operating rental properties can involve a lot of chaos. Your perfect tenant suddenly decides to start selling crack. Even though your lease states "NO PETS", your new tenant has a pit bull. A tenant is so filthy that 50,000 cockroaches now inhabit your beautiful, newly rehabbed house. All these things and more happen with regularity. I've had every one of these things happen AND WORSE! When these incidents occur, will you be able to sleep at night or will it drive you crazy? Not everyone can deal with this crap!

5. Are you willing to risk your money and your credit?

    If you are going to be a landlord, then you will be risking your money and your credit. It is a statistical fact that the majority of people who start a new business fail in a short period of time. Are you willing to risk your money and your credit to start a rental business?

6. Could you evict a young mother with her newborn child because she did not pay the rent on time?

    Here it is… the big question! This is something that you will almost certainly face. If you can not bring yourself to quickly evict tenants when they don't pay, you will not make it as a landlord. Many tenants are also professional victims. They always have an excuse and they prey on the sympathy of kind-hearted landlords. If you can not evict someone for not paying, seek another business.

7. Are you willing to deal with drug dealers and drug addicts occasionally?

    Unfortunately, dealing with drug dealers, addicts, thieves, drunks, and other criminals is an all too frequent part of this business. Regardless of how well you screen the tenants and what other precautions you take, you will eventually have a drug dealer living in one of your properties. I have had this happen several times and it is no fun. In almost every case, you will have to evict these people and they will not like it. I have been threatened on several occasions and these tenants can be dangerous. One of the drug dealers that I recently evicted was just arrested for trying to shoot a junkie for not paying a $20 bill for crack. This did not happen in a war zone in a big city ghetto, this happened right here in my little corner of Ohio!

8. Are you willing to testify in court (for evictions, lawsuits, crimes)?

    I often joke that I spend more time in court than the judge! Thankfully, that's not quite true, but sometimes it seems like that. As a landlord, you'll probably be evicting about 1% of your tenants each month. I've never heard this mentioned by any guru, but realize that this will happen. See you in court!

9. Do you deal well with conflict?

   Conflict is part of this job. The tenants will be perpetually testing you and they will be mad when you won't give in to their wishes. If you need everyone to like you and be your friend, then you'll be disappointed by this business. In fact, I can almost guarantee that you will make some enemies in this business.

10. Can you do some of the maintenance yourself?

   This is not mandatory, but it will save you a lot of money. You don't need to be a jack of all trades, but you will make more money if you can learn a few simple maintenance tasks. For example, a typical plumber charges about $75 per hour and they often have a minimum service charge. If you can spend 15 minutes fixing a leaking toilet, a dripping faucet, or a clogged sink a few times a month, you will save a lot of money. You see, with rentals you get all the money at the beginning of the month and then see how much you can keep. The more you can do, the more you will make.

This exercise has been entirely for your benefit. You may very well have found a few areas that you think will be difficult for you. You should take an honest look in the mirror and decide if you can overcome these obstacles.

Nothing is worth being miserable all the time. I have met landlords who were absolutely sick as the result of dealing with tenants. The stress can be enormous if you have the wrong personality or the wrong expectations. Many people find it extremely stressful to evict a tenant and to have tenants mad at them. These are simply parts of the business.

There is some good news. Human beings can become accustomed to almost anything. With a little time and a lot of persistence, you can overcome your weak areas and become a successful landlord. Use this personality test to determine if you want to try.

BUSINESS PLAN

Proper **P**rior **P**lanning **P**revents **P**ainfully **P**oor **P**erformance! Those are the 7 P's of success in any endeavor. Successful entrepreneurs know that nothing could be more important when it comes to starting a business than proper planning. Let me be absolutely clear about one thing - operating rental properties IS A BUSINESS - not an investment. A popular definition of the word "investment" is: 'committing money to a venture in hopes of a future return'. Investments are things like stocks and bank CDs. Investments are completely passive ways to make money, you pay your money and wait for results. You'll notice that this definition does not include the words WORK or TIME. Starting a business requires not only money, but a lot of your work and a lot of your time.

"80% of new businesses fail in a short period of time". We've all heard that statistic. Almost all of these businesses fail because they run out of cash. They simply don't have sufficient cash flow to pay the bills and feed the owner. One of the biggest reasons that these new businesses did not have the proper cash flow is that they did not create a business plan that would ensure that the proper cash flow could be maintained by the business. The owner just started the business hoping that things would be alright. Unfortunately, hope is not a good substitute for a well thought-out plan!

Starting a business should involve a high probability of success. Thinking through all aspects of your business in advance is one way to help increase your chance of success. A business plan is nothing more than a written explanation of every aspect of your new business.

Rich

Everyone wants to be rich. Certainly, many people who enter the rental property business do so with the intent of becoming rich. If that is your goal, then you should decide exactly what "rich" means to you. Do you want to have a net worth of a million dollars? Do you want to make $10,000 per month in profit? Do you want to have one million dollars in cash? What exactly is your goal? Write your goal on the following lines:

My goal is _____

_____

_____

1 MINUTE TO RENTAL PROPERTY RICHES

Now that you've identified your personal goal, you need to write a business plan that will ensure that you meet your goal. Whatever you goal, it is possible to achieve it with rental properties. You just need to decide on a business model that will make that happen.

For example, let's say that your goal was to make $10,000 per month. Let's assume that you can buy rental properties in your area that will give you a positive cash flow (profit) of $100 each per month. Therefore, to make $10,000 per month, you would need 100 rentals! We now know what we need to reach our goal (100 rentals with a monthly cash flow of $100 per month) and we can write a business plan to achieve this goal.

In a similar fashion, if our goal was to have a net worth of $1,000,000 from our rental property business, we would need to know the average equity that we could expect from each property we buy. If we could buy the average property at a $10,000 discount, then it would take 100 properties to acquire one million dollars of equity (net worth).

Business Plan Basics

A business plan does not need to be a very long and involved document. In fact, business plans can range from a few notes scrawled on the back of a napkin to a multiple-volume document for a large national corporation. Fortunately, a business plan for a small rental property business need not be too long or complicated.

There are at least two reasons to develop a business plan. As already described, the first reason is to create a roadmap for your new business. The second reason is to create a document that can be given to banks, other investors, and potential partners. Your business plan will tell others what your business is all about and show them that you are serious about your business.

On the following 5 pages you will find my personal business plan. You may find that it meets your needs or you may modify it as needed to reflect your new business.

REAL ESTATE BUSINESS PLAN

OF

Your Name Here

Date:_____

Copy # _____ of _____

THIS DOCUMENT CONTAINS CONFIDENTIAL AND PRIVILEGED INFORMATION INTENDED ONLY FOR USE BY:

_____[Name]
_____[Company]

Real Estate Business Plan

Introduction

This business plan was developed to provide a clear and concise framework for establishing a successful real estate business. In its most basic form, our real estate business shall consist of purchasing properties at a discounted price, rehabbing the properties as necessary, and renting the properties in a profitable manner.

Objectives

There are three objectives in establishing this real estate business:

    1) to provide a stream of passive income for our family,
    2) to rapidly build equity in various properties, and
    3) to establish a real estate based source of retirement.

Method

To meet our objectives, we will follow a four part plan:

    1) Locate and Purchase Properties at a Discount

To locate properties at a discount, we will concentrate on finding sellers that are desperate to get rid of their properties. Desperate sellers can include landlords with problem tenants, foreclosures, estate sales, people involved in divorce, out-of-town owners, and people with depressed properties. In addition, properties that have been on the market for over 90 days and bank-owned properties offer excellent opportunities to buy properties at a discount.

    2) Rehab/Renovate the Properties

We will rehab houses to the extent necessary to attract quality tenants. Every aspect of each house must be clean, safe, fully functional, and attractive.

    3) Screen Potential Tenants

We fully understand that attracting high quality tenants is a critical step in our business plan. To find these tenants, we will perform a credit check, criminal background check, and check references on every potential tenant. Only those applicants with a good payment history, little or no criminal history, and excellent references will be considered as tenants.

4) Generate a Positive Cash Flow

Our policy will be that EVERY property that we own must generate a positive cash flow after ALL expenses are paid. A cash flow analysis of every potential property purchase will be made to ensure that the property will produce a positive cash flow.

By following this four step plan, we will generate income in five distinct ways:

1) Immediate Equity

We will purchase all properties at a discount, which will result in our acquiring instant equity in the property at the time of purchase. Our goal will be to purchase properties at 70% or less of Fair Market Value (FMV). Fair Market Value will be determined by using appraisals, comparative market analysis, and most importantly through familiarity with the local real estate market.

2) Positive Cash Flow

Each property will generate a positive cash flow, which will provide income that can be used to further expand the business.

3) Loan Balance Pay-down

Mortgages and Loans will be paid down over time using the rents from the tenants. Our basic strategy will be to obtain mortgages and commercial loans with competitive interest rates and a 20 year term. However, the overriding consideration will be a mortgage rate and term that will allow all expenses to be paid and a positive cash flow to be maintained. Interest only and negative amortization loans will not be used.

4) Property Appreciation

Statistically, properties in the United States have appreciated at an average rate of 3% to 5% per year over the past 20 years. By utilizing our buy and hold (rental) strategy, we will benefit from this appreciation in real estate values over time.

5) Tax Implications

Finally, we will generate additional income by reducing taxes through depreciation and write-offs. We will aggressively pursue these tax gains by utilizing a professional to prepare our taxes and advise us on tax matters.

Concept and Market Niche

After researching the real estate rental market in our area, we determined that there was a shortage of high quality, clean housing at reasonable rental rates. There is also a shortage of units for the Section 8 program (government paid housing). Therefore, our niche will be to rent high-quality, clean, and attractive housing to both private and government paid tenants after a thorough screening.

Marketing

We will use classified ads in the local newspaper to market our rental units to potential tenants. In order to maximize income, we will begin advertising approximately 2 weeks before rehabilitation is estimated to be complete. Advertising on this time schedule will permit us to have tenants in the housing as it is completed and ready for occupancy.

Growth

We realize that it is important to grow in a controlled, steady manner. To this end, it will be our goal to acquire 10 rental units each year. Initially, we will acquire single family houses because these units are the easiest to rent and sell. After acquiring at least 5 single family houses, we may also begin to acquire duplexes and triplexes as they become available. These multi-unit houses often offer greater profit margins per unit, but are more risky investments because they are more difficult to sell and often attract a lower quality tenant. Once we acquire 20 units, we may begin to acquire apartment buildings, but we will limit our units in apartment buildings to 50% of our total units owned.

Management Philosophy

Our management philosophy can be summarized by the phrase "FAIR and FIRM". This phrase means that we will treat all of our tenants fairly, but we will insist that all terms of the lease are met. Non-paying tenants will be immediately evicted. To minimize risk and maximize tenant satisfaction, we will rapidly address maintenance problems and other tenant issues.

Building a Team

Every successful business consists of at least one team of key people. Our team will include a real estate agent, small local banks, private investors, an appraiser, a title agency, various tradesmen, and maintenance personnel. It is our goal to find team members that are professional, reliable, honest, and that can participate and share in our future success.

Organizational Structure

In order to limit liability, we will divide our real estate holdings into multiple legal entities. Initially, we will place five rental units into each entity. After accumulating twenty total units in four entities, we will begin increasing the number of rental units in each entity until we have twenty units per entity. Upon reaching twenty units per entity, we will re-evaluate the organizational structure and decide how to proceed from that point.

Diversification

Initially, it will be advantageous to accumulate houses in our local area. This is an advantage because we have an intimate knowledge of our local real estate market and will be able to easily manage and control our properties. Once we reach a total of twenty rental units, then we will consider diversifying to neighboring towns to lower our risk of a downturn in a single rental market.

Continuing Education

Continuing education is important in every profession. It shall be the policy of our business to allocate funds for education of our personnel. This education will take the form of various books, tapes, seminars, conventions, workshops, and other educational programs.

Summary

The objective of our real estate business is to provide equity and income for our family. To meet this objective, we will utilize our team to locate discounted properties; rehab the properties as needed; and find quality tenants to rent them. This will result in generating a positive cash flow from each property. We will establish a market niche by renting clean, quality properties at a reasonable price. All of our tenants will be treated in a "Fair and Firm" manner. Our business will grow in a controlled and steady manner and will diversify as we grow to ensure added safety. Finally, we will continue our real estate education over time so that we can take advantage of new ideas and innovations.

BUYING RIGHT

The success of your rental property business will be made or lost <u>when you buy</u> your rental properties. It is often said that 'you make your money in real estate when you buy.' This is VERY true. But...first things first! Before you buy anything, there is a LOT of work to do.

Education

Your first step on the road to landlording success needs to be education. You need to know everything about your business, from locating properties to evicting tenants. Don't worry, I'm not trying to sell you something else! In fact, I strongly believe that you can get all the real estate education you need for very little money.

The book that you are reading covers everything from A to Z about buying and operating rental properties, but after completing this book and maybe even re-reading it 2 or 3 times, you should aggressively continue your education.

There are many excellent books about real estate investing. I would recommend reading as many as you can. Even one idea that you pick up from a book can make you thousands of dollars in this business. Therefore, I consider the time required to read these books to be time well spent. Start you own investing library.

In addition to books, there are many real estate "gurus" out there selling courses. Many of these courses contain good information, but you must remember that these gurus make their money upselling their students to the next level course or seminar. In addition, many of these courses and seminars are quite expensive and don't provide any better information than can be found in a good book. One other caveat is that the gurus often provide only the most optimistic scenarios. In my experience, very few gurus discuss the actual expenses that you will encounter. If you were to believe their expense numbers as they relate to rental properties, you could quickly find yourself losing a LOT of money.

Many of the Gurus also offer coaching and mentoring programs which are usually VERY expensive. I do not recommend coaching or mentoring from the gurus unless you are receiving one-on-one training from the guru himself. Many of these coaching and mentoring programs provide an instructor who is nothing more than an employee reading from a script book. You don't need that!

Here's one final consideration regarding expensive courses, coaching, and mentoring. It is my observation that most successful entrepreneurs are self-starters. They can read and absorb information without the need to be spoon fed. If you don't have this trait, you might want to seriously consider whether real estate investing is for you.

Real Estate Investors Association (REIA)

If you are planning to be a successful landlord, you should belong to your local Real Estate Investors Association (REIA) or real estate investor's club. At the REIA, you will find other local investors who are eager to share information with you. This is an educational source that you can not find anywhere else and it is free (or very low cost). Your job is to determine who the successful investors are and make some new friends. These people know all about your local real estate market, rental property issues, political issues, local taxes, local eviction procedures, and much, much more!

One word of caution about the REIA: do NOT hang around with other newbies! What you'll find at the REIA is that there is an ever changing large group of newbies at each meeting. As a newbie yourself, it is very tempting to simply hang around with the other newbies. Don't do this. Your goal is to be a successful Landlord. Therefore, you need to hang around with other successful landlords.

Internet

There is a lot of good information to be found on the internet. Many real estate related websites, newsgroups, message boards, and mailing lists exist that can be an excellent source of information. In addition, there are an almost infinite number of books, e-books, courses, products and other materials available for purchase.

Caution! Anyone can pretend to be anything on the internet. The VAST majority of people on the various real estate sites are newbies. All the information that you find on the web should be viewed with a reasonable amount of suspicion. Much of the advice found on the web is WRONG. In addition, there is an entire industry of people trying to take advantage of new real estate investors. As a rule, I would not become involved in any real estate deals with persons that I met on the internet.

1 MINUTE TO RENTAL PROPERTY RICHES

Learning Your Market

Ladies and gentlemen, please fasten your seatbelts! You are now ready to begin your journey to becoming a successful real estate investor. Your first step is to learn your LOCAL market. In fact, I want you to become an EXPERT in your local market.

Why do I say LOCAL market? Because IT IS NEARLY IMPOSSIBLE TO MAKE MONEY WITH RENTALS LONG DISTANCE! It is hard enough to make a profit with rentals when you buy locally and do all the management and maintenance yourself. In my opinion, trying to start a real estate investing business long distance is financial suicide.

Now that we've decided that you'll be investing in your own community, you need to become an expert in that local market. The first thing you need to do is identify the area that you'll be investing in. With rentals, you will normally be buying lower to moderate priced houses. On the high end, these are working class neighborhoods. On the lower end, these are the rougher areas of town where the majority of people live on government assistance. Ironically, the higher cash flows are often found in the lower end properties. Do NOT buy properties in areas where you are afraid to drive during the day. We certainly do not want to buy properties in War Zones - areas where bullets fly on a regular basis!

So, how do you find your target area? There are a couple of easy methods. First, you can look in your local newspaper's classified ad section for rentals. See where the majority of rentals are located. Second, you can drive around your town looking for "For Rent' signs. In good rental neighborhoods, a large percentage of the houses will be rentals. Again, these are working class and lower class neighborhoods.

Once you've picked an area that you're interested in, your assignment is to become an expert in that area. To do that, you MUST get out there and look at houses. Drive around the neighborhood and look for "Open House", "For Sale by Owner", and "For Sale" signs. Write down the phone numbers, call them, and arrange to go see them (inside and out). Go see at least 50 houses in your target area. Looking at 100 would be even better. The point is that you should keep looking at houses until you can tell what the house is worth just by looking at it. If you need to look at 200 houses to become this proficient, then do it. DO WHATEVER IT TAKES! This is where the wannabes are separated from the future successful landlords. If you won't invest the time to take this step, then you will almost surely fail and I would suggest that you quit NOW!

1 MINUTE TO RENTAL PROPERTY RICHES

Market Trends - Nationally and Locally

After looking at 50, 100, or 200 houses and becoming intimately familiar with property values in your target area, you need to determine what the trend is for both your local market and nationally. Are property values increasing? Decreasing? Stable? Is the economy improving or headed downhill? Is the country headed into a recession or rapidly growing? How is your local community doing? Are companies moving into or out of the area? Is there a great demand for rental properties or is the vacancy rate very high? Are rents increasing or decreasing? What is your local unemployment rate? Ok, Ok, you get the idea!

Where will you find the answers to all these questions? Start with other successful investors (hint: you'll find them at your REIA). Read the local newspaper. Look up information on the internet. Again, do whatever it takes to understand the trends that will affect your business! The more informed you are - the more successful you will be.

Houses vs. Apartments

There are many choices available to the rental property investor. You can choose to buy single family houses, duplexes, small apartment buildings, or apartment complexes.

In my opinion, this choice is very easy. I would strongly urge you to start your landlording career with single family houses (SFHs). There are a myriad of reasons for starting with single family houses:

1. There is a very large supply of single family houses available at all times.
2. Most people are familiar with single family houses and therefore it makes sense to start with something you are familiar with.
3. If you discover that being a landlord is not for you, single family houses are much easier to sell than multi-unit apartment buildings.
4. The tenants that rent single family houses are generally better, more stable tenants.
5. Doing one single family rental at a time allows you to gradually adjust to dealing with tenants and therefore start your landlording career with a better experience.

1 MINUTE TO RENTAL PROPERTY RICHES

Buying at a Discount - The 70% Rule

As I've already said, it is nearly impossible to buy a property at retail and then rent it for a profit. My rule is that I will not pay more than 70% of the market value for a property, less the repair costs.

For example, let's say that we find a rental property that we feel might be worth buying. We have looked at over 100 houses in our target area and we know that the market value of this house should be $50,000. We have thoroughly inspected the house and believe that $5,000 in repairs are needed to make this house rentable. So, based on our 70% rule, our maximum purchase price would be $30,000. Let's look at the math:

Market Value	$50,000
(multiplied by .7)	x .70
	= $35,000
Minus Repairs	- $ 5,000
Maximum Purchase Price	= $30,000

So, based only on our 70% rule, our maximum purchase price for this property would be $30,000. You will note that if we follow this rule, we will have at least 30% equity with every house we buy, even after we make repairs. In this case, if we bought this house, we would have $15,000 in instant equity (after repairs)!

There are a couple of reasons that we MUST buy at a discount.

1. Picking up this instant equity helps us build wealth, which is one of the five ways that we're making money with rentals.

2. This equity is our "insurance policy" in case things go wrong. For example, let's say that you buy the house and a few months later discover that you absolutely hate dealing with tenants. You can't sleep at night and the entire thing has been a nightmare. You want OUT! If you had paid full price, the house could be difficult to sell because you will need to sell at full market price just to break even. If the market has declined since you bought the house, it might be impossible to sell the property without taking a loss. However, you were smart and followed the 70% rule. You can sell the house at a price below market value and still make a profit. Even if the market has declined, you have a 30% cushion that ensures you can get out without taking a loss. **BUYING AT A DISCOUNT IS IMPERATIVE!**

Page 31

© 2006 Ciara International, Inc. - All Rights Reserved   www.1minutetorentalpropertyriches.com

CASH FLOW

What is cash flow? Very simply, cash flow is the money left over after all expenses are paid. Without proper cash flow, your business will certainly fail. It is just that simple!

CASHFLOW IS THE LIFEBLOOD OF EVERY BUSINESS.

To be able to have an intelligent discussion of cash flow, we first need to define some terms. I am defining these terms as they apply to rental properties.

1. Gross Rent - this is the rent that you receive from your tenants each month.

2. Operating Expenses - are those expenses that you must pay EXCLUDING your mortgage payment (principal and interest only). The mortgage payment is often referred to as Debt or Debt Service. With rentals, operating expenses include taxes, insurance, maintenance, management, vacancies, legal expenses, eviction expenses, court costs, exterminations, capital expenses (replacement of major items like the roof, heating and air conditioning, etc), lawsuits, office expenses, fuel for you vehicle, damage caused by tenants, advertising, and much, much more.

3. Net Operating Income (NOI) - is Gross Rent minus Operating Expenses.

4. Debt or Debt Service - is the principle and interest (mortgage) payment on the property.

5. Cash Flow - is Gross Rent minus Operating Expenses and Debt Service. This is the same as saying that cash flow is Net Operating Income minus Debt Service. You will note that cash flow can either be positive or negative. A positive cash flow means that you are making money. A negative cash flow means that you are losing money and that your business will fail unless the situation is corrected.

Now that we've defined the basic terms, let's discuss how to evaluate a property for positive cash flow. This is one of the most misunderstood issues by new landlords and the one that is chiefly responsible for the vast majority of new landlords failing. **In fact, the absolute lack of accurate information on this subject is exactly why I decided to write this book.**

1 MINUTE TO RENTAL PROPERTY RICHES

I have attended dozens of presentations by some of the nation's leading real estate "gurus". Not one guru even came close to accurately discussing the expenses that landlords will incur - NOT ONE!

Typically, the gurus will instruct their students to determine cash flow with a formula like this:

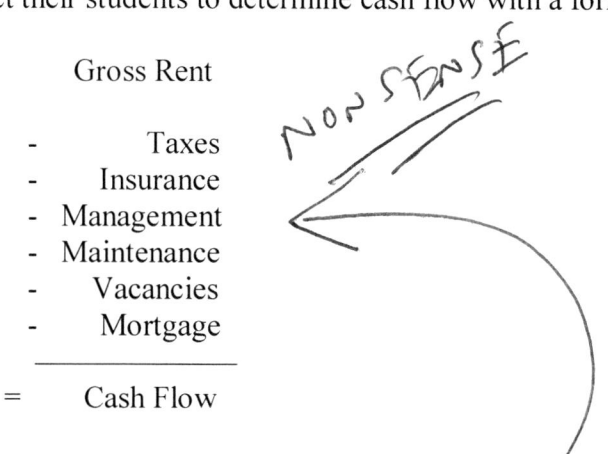

Gross Rent
- Taxes
- Insurance
- Management
- Maintenance
- Vacancies
- Mortgage
―――――
= Cash Flow

[Handwritten annotation: "NONSENSE" with arrow pointing to formula]

This formula seems to make sense and it is easy to calculate. Taxes and insurance are easily determined. Management companies usually charge about 10% of the gross rent. You can use an estimate for Maintenance and Vacancies (many gurus use about 5% of gross rent for each of these expenses).

When I entered into this business, I BELIEVED THIS NONSENSE! I read dozens of books. I attended many guru presentations and they were all saying it. I BELIEVED IT! The only problem is that this method of determining cash flow is blatantly WRONG! I don't know how to say it any more simply. The gurus either didn't know what they were talking about or they were lying! Is that blunt enough?

My realization that I had been misled was slow in coming. My goal was to buy 50 rentals in 5 years. To reach that goal, my business plan was to purchase 10 rentals per year and that is exactly what I did. In fact, things went so well that I actually exceeded this goal. Even so, it took about 2 years to fully realize that the guru numbers were badly flawed.

During my first year as a landlord, I did not have a single vacancy and not a single tenant that caused any trouble. Beginner's luck I suppose. I thought that I had discovered the pot of gold at the end of the rainbow! It seemed so easy! It WAS so easy! I thought that I was a genius!

WRONG!

© 2006 Ciara International, Inc. - All Rights Reserved   www.1minutetorentalpropertyriches.com

1 MINUTE TO RENTAL PROPERTY RICHES

As my portfolio of rental properties grew, things began to change. As their one-year leases ended, some of the tenants in my original rentals left. I had vacancies for the first time. Although these vacancies started to eat away at my self-awarded genius status, the gurus had included vacancies in their cash flow analysis. So far, so good.

Time continued to pass and my portfolio continued to grow per my business plan. Something strange started to happen. I had an eviction, then another. Now my cash flow projections were beginning to fall short. The gurus did not say anything about evictions. Here in my little corner of Ohio, filing an eviction costs $136. My lawyer charges $150 per eviction. Once the eviction is granted, it costs $308 to "set out" the tenants. The setout is where the court bailiff actually moves all the tenant's stuff to the curb and physically kicks them out. It takes AT LEAST 5 weeks to complete the eviction, which from a practical point means that you'll have at least 2 months of vacancies. While we are talking about evictions, VERY FEW evicted tenants leave the property in great shape. The damage can be nothing more than a bunch of trash to be cleaned up, but all too often the tenants intentionally do damage to the property - SOMETIMES A LOT OF DAMAGE!

It was at this point that I began to realize that the "GURU" cash flow formulas were all wrong! They only included the most basic expenses in their formula. I was not a genius at all. In fact, I felt a little foolish that I had been stupid enough to believe these gurus. Should it not have occurred to me that I would have evictions and that the gurus had failed to include these expenses in their formulas? Should I not have realized that I would have legal expenses? Should I not have thought about office expenses? Should I not have anticipated the fuel for my pickup truck that takes me to and from my rentals? Suddenly, I felt more like an IDIOT than a genius!

It is at this point that the majority of new investors are forced out of business with a big loss of money. Fortunately, I had done one thing right! I purchased all of my houses at a huge discount! In fact, my average purchase price was only about 61% of market value. Even with all these unanticipated operating expenses, my debt payment was so low that I was still making money! The bad news was that I was only making about half of my predicted positive cash flow. The good news was that I was profitable! Buying right had saved my business!

I discussed this issue with several other successful investors. ALL of them had experienced the same thing and they all knew that the guru numbers were bogus. The difficulty was in trying to come up with a formula that takes into account all of the expenses that I had incurred as well as others that I had yet to incur. How could you anticipate which property would have an eviction, a lawsuit, or excessive damage caused by a tenant in any given year? YOU CAN'T. Obviously, I wasn't the first person ever to discover that there were a myriad of expenses that the gurus omitted. There had to be an answer.

1 MINUTE TO RENTAL PROPERTY RICHES

As it turned out, there are many surveys of operating expenses out there. The National Apartment Association is one example of a group that has published these numbers. There are many other sources available also, and I invite you to do some research on this topic. The bottom line is that throughout the United States, operating expenses run 45% to 50% of gross rents. Since I want to be very conservative with my cash flow calculation, I'll use 50%.

Let's review. Cash flow is found by subtracting operating expenses and the mortgage payment from the gross rents. Operating expenses are all of the expenses that you encounter EXCEPT the mortgage payment (which is also called debt service). Operating expenses include things such as taxes, insurance, maintenance, management, vacancies, legal fees, attorney fees, evictions, court costs, exterminations, utilities paid by the owner, office supplies, a computer used for your business, ink for your printer, set-out fees, fuel for your vehicle, cleaning expenses, lawsuits, capital expenses (major purchases and repairs), and anything else that you must pay as the property owner EXCEPT the mortgage payment (principal and interest).

We've discovered that all of these operating expenses add up to 50% (1/2) of the gross rents. Therefore, since 1/2 of the gross rent is used to pay operating expenses, that leaves 1/2 of the gross rents with which to pay the mortgage and have some positive cash flow, also called profit.

Therefore, the following is our cash flow formula:

$$\begin{aligned} &\text{1/2 of Gross Rents} \\ &\underline{-\ \text{Mortgage Payment (principal and interest)}} \\ &=\ \ \text{Cash Flow} \end{aligned}$$

This formula is VERY simple and much more accurate than the "guru" formulas. It accounts for all of the expenses that you should expect to incur. The data that created this formula came from the experience of hundreds of thousands of real world investors. This is the cash flow formula that I use!

My rule is that for lower-priced rentals, those costing less than $50,000, I must have at least $100 per rental unit per month in positive cash flow USING THE ABOVE FORMULA.

1 MINUTE TO RENTAL PROPERTY RICHES

Let's take another look at our cash flow formula:

1/2 of Gross Rents

- Mortgage Payment (principal and interest)
_____

= Cash Flow

You'll remember that the reason that the top line of our formula is "1/2 of Gross Rents" is that the other 1/2 of the gross rents went to pay operating expenses. So, we could rewrite this formula to look like this:

Gross Rents

- 1/2 of Gross Rents (operating expenses)

- Mortgage Payment (principal and interest)
_____

= Cash Flow

[handwritten note: WE CAN lower this !!!]

So, based on this formula, what can you do to increase your cash flow. There are 3 things:

1. You could increase Gross Rents
2. You could decrease Operating Expenses
3. You could decrease the Mortgage Payment

Let's examine each one:

1. Increasing Gross Rents - it is difficult to increase Gross Rents because rents are set primarily by the supply and demand of the area. If you increase rents above market rates, your tenants will leave and you'll have a negative cash flow.

   There is one way that you can increase the Gross Rents a little. You could improve your property so that it is in greater demand. For example, if none of the other rentals in your neighborhood have a garage, you might add a garage. With a garage, there would be greater demand for your property and you could probably raise the rent. The question is whether the improvement will generate enough extra income to cover the expense of building the garage. This same principle could apply to any improvement that you make, including painting, new carpet, a dishwasher, etc.

1 MINUTE TO RENTAL PROPERTY RICHES

2. You Could Decrease Operating Expenses - but making a significant difference in the operating expenses is very difficult. Many of the operating expenses are either fixed costs or unpredictable.

   There are some expenses that you have almost no control over. A few examples are property taxes, damage done by tenants, evictions, court costs, and legal fees.

   Other expenses offer you some limited control. Examples of this type of expense might be insurance and vacancies. You could shop around for insurance to get a better price. How many dollars per month would this save you? Probably not many. The same is true of vacancies. You could institute a tenant retention program and give all of your tenants a gift on the anniversary of their lease. How many tenants will stay another year because of a $50 gift? In my experience, tenants are very fickle. They don't think far into the future. The presence of a small gift would make little difference in whether a tenant stays or goes.

3. You Could Decrease Your Mortgage Payment - BINGO! This is the one area that can make a significant difference in your cash flow. So, how do we lower the mortgage payment? There are several ways:

- You can negotiate a lower interest rate with your lender. This is probably the least effective method of lowering your mortgage payment, because interest rates are set by the market and by your credit score. You can not control the market and you can not quickly change your credit score (although improving your credit score is a good idea).

- You can change the length of your loan. Changing from a 15 year to 30 year loan will have an effect on the mortgage payment. For example, a $50,000 loan at 7% interest for 15 years has a mortgage payment of $449 per month. The same $50,000 loan at 7% for 30 years has a mortgage payment of $333 per month. That's a $116 per month difference. The only problem here is that most people are already using a 30 year mortgage.

YOU CAN LOWER THE AMOUNT BORROWED. I'm sure that you noticed the bold print on this one. **This is the number one way that you can increase your cash flow!** To lower the amount borrowed you can either make a large downpayment or buy the property at a bigger discount. For most investors, putting a large downpayment on many rental properties will quickly deplete their valuable cash. Therefore, the very best thing that you can do to increase your cash flow is to buy the property at a BIG discount. I can not over-emphasize how important it is to buy all your rental properties at a discount! Buying at a discount not only improves your cash flow but it also gives you instant equity.

ALWAYS BUY AT A DISCOUNT

1 MINUTE TO RENTAL PROPERTY RICHES

Do It Yourself to EARN Extra Cash Flow

There is one more thing that we can do to EARN extra cash flow from our rental properties. We can perform the management and maintenance work ourselves. It is important to understand that doing this work does not really change our cash flow, because we still have management and maintenance expenses. However, WE are earning these management and maintenance fees instead of paying someone else to do them.

For a typical rental, professional managers charge about 10% of the gross rents. In addition, paid managers often charge an extra fee for placing tenants and yet another fee for arranging maintenance. By the time you have paid all of these fees, the manager can easily be taking 15% of your gross rents. If your property rents for $600 per month, the management fees can easily be eating up $90 per month. This is money that YOU could be making.

This same tactic can be used with the maintenance. Hiring out maintenance can be EXTREMELY expensive. The most common maintenance issues all deal with water. Leaking toilets, leaking water lines, and dripping sinks are the most common maintenance complaints. These complaints are very easily fixed (usually in only a few minutes) with only common hand tools and a little knowledge. However, if you call a plumber to take care of these issues, you'll be lucky to have even the simplest complaint fixed for less than $100. If you can do the maintenance repairs yourself, then you will earn this extra money.

What if you don't know how to do these maintenance tasks? LEARN! When I first started my rental property business, I did not know how to do virtually any of these maintenance tasks. I had never changed a toilet. I had never repaired plaster. I had never replaced a door. I had never installed carpet. Now, I am proficient at all of these maintenance tasks and many, many more. In fact, I can completely rehab a property and do all the work myself with only one exception, heating and air-conditioning. Although I have not tackled heating and air-conditioning yet, that may be in the future!

How do you learn to do the maintenance? You could go to Lowes or Home Depot and buy a home repair book. These books have easy to follow instructions and a lot of pictures. The big home improvement stores also offer free classes in common home repair tasks. Taking advantage of these free classes is an excellent way to learn. You could also ask a friend who is a handyman to help you. If you don't feel comfortable with either of these methods, then hire someone to help you the first time or two. Doing the maintenance yourself will save (earn) you a bunch of money.

1 MINUTE TO RENTAL PROPERTY RICHES

The 2% Rule

There is a third rule that I use to screen properties for potential purchase. That rule is called the 2% Rule. This rule says that you should look for properties that have gross rents of at least 2% of the cost of the property. The cost of the property is the purchase price plus any needed repairs.

Here's an example. You are thinking about buying the following property to be a rental:

Asking Price: $50,000
Expected Gross Rent: $650

Therefore, we divide $650 by $50,000 to get .013, which is 1.3%. Since 1.3% is lower than 2%, this property does not meet our 2% rule and therefore is probably not worth buying as a rental.

Question: how much could we pay for this house for it to meet our 2% rule.

To find the answer, simply divide the gross rent by .02 (which is 2%).

$$\$650 / .02 = \$32,500.$$

So, using our 2% rule, the maximum that we could pay for this property would be $32,500.

Summary of Rental Property Purchase Rules

1. Maximum purchase price should be 70% or less of market value if no repairs are needed. If repairs are needed, calculate 70% of the market price and then subtract the repairs to determine the maximum purchase price.

2. The minimum positive cash flow from any property we buy should be $100 per unit per month for houses costing less than $50,000. We determine the cash flow by subtracting the mortgage payment from 1/2 of the gross rent. For properties costing more than $50,000, raise the minimum positive cash flow as desired.

3. Buy only properties that generate gross rents of 2% of the cost of the property (purchase price plus repairs).

LOCATING RENTAL PROPERTIES

There are many ways to locate properties that would make good rentals. Entire books and courses have been written on this subject. I do not pretend to give you an in-depth look at every possible way to find properties in this book. My intent is to give you a basic look at some highly successful methods of locating rentals. I encourage you to continue your education after reading this book.

Locating rental properties doesn't need to be complicated or expensive. Likewise, it does not need to involve a highly complicated or elaborate marketing program. Many times, the most simple and traditional methods of finding properties are the best!

Real Estate Agents

Believe it or not, one of my most profitable ways to find properties has been to use a real estate agent. The key is to find a hungry real estate agent that is willing to work with an investor. When I first started my rental business, I starting using real estate agents. I went through two agents before I finally found one that was anxious to work with me. She was very young and had just recently gotten her real estate license. She was hungry for business and willing to work hard to find great deals for me. I have bought a bunch of deals through this agent and she continues to bring me great deals today.

One word of caution when dealing with agents. They work on commission and don't want to waste their time running wannabes all over town looking at properties that they can't or won't buy. Therefore, even though you are a new investor, you need to be prepared to buy a property if the agent finds one that meets your criteria.

At your first meeting, sit down with the agent and give her a written copy of your purchasing criteria. Explain that you only want to see properties that meet your criteria and that you WILL buy when she finds an appropriate property. You may also want to explain that you will be buying several properties a year and you will use her exclusively if she does a good job.

Since you will be buying really cheap properties, reward the agent by giving her a bonus if she finds you a great property at a really low price. Remember that the agent is working on commission and therefore the commission on a really cheap property will be very low, often too low to make it worthwhile. Giving a bonus for great performance also builds loyalty and will increase the number of deals that come your way.

1 MINUTE TO RENTAL PROPERTY RICHES

REOs (Real Estate Owned by the Bank)

At the time this book is being written in October 2006, the real estate bubble has begun deflating. The nationwide rapid price appreciation of the past few years has come to a screeching halt and the average time on the market has drastically increased. The inventory of houses for sale has increased tremendously and housing prices have just begun to fall.

My research indicates that the downward leg of the real estate cycle after a major boom takes about two years. Therefore, I believe that we won't hit bottom until early 2008. My research also indicates that it could take another 8 to 10 years for prices to once again return to the previous inflation adjusted highs. In other words, my prediction is that we won't completely recover from this downturn until about 2016.

During the real estate boom, real estate prices became irrationally high. In many "HOT" markets, new investors bought property as fast as it came on the market. People actually camped out in some markets just to have the chance to bid on pre-construction projects. This is the same irrational exuberance that existed in the stock market 5 years before.

The frenzy that surrounded the real estate fad extended to the lending industry. Lending standards were relaxed to the point that just about all that was needed to get a loan was someone with a pulse. Adjustable rate mortgages (ARMs), option ARMs, negative amortization loans, and other dangerous products became the norm. It seemed that everyone jumped on the bandwagon and bought a house, including millions of people with terrible credit. These new homeowners were the working poor who normally would be renters.

Millions of these working poor homeowners have neither the income or the financial discipline to be homeowners. Unfortunately, they will be losing their homes to foreclosure over the next few years. This trend has already started. Additionally, millions of new real estate investors will fail during the next few years resulting in an explosion of foreclosures.

Most of these foreclosed properties will end up being owned by the banks as REOs (Real Estate Owned by the bank). Banks do not want to own these properties and in many cases will sell them at a big discount to get them off their books.

To find out about REOs, you need a real estate agent. The banks list their REOs with a realtor as soon as they become available for sale. If you have a real estate agent working for you as I suggested in the last section, you should receive a call as soon as these properties come on the market.

1 MINUTE TO RENTAL PROPERTY RICHES

Buying REOs is a little different than buying a property from an individual. The following list identifies some of the differences that you'll find with REOs.

- Banks will require the buyer to have proof of funds or a loan pre-approval from a lender.
- Banks normally will not accept many (or any) contingencies in the contract.
- Banks will often require a significant deposit.
- Banks will often have a penalty clause in their contract that charges the buyer for each day that the deal is late in closing.
- Banks do not respect any deadlines that you put in your offer.
- Banks often will "shop" your offer to other buyers in an effort to get a better price.
- Banks are often willing to hold onto the property for months rather than selling it at a discount.

In other words, banks are very difficult to work with. You can take some comfort in knowing that you are not the only one frustrated in these REO deals. Your realtor makes her money by closing deals. She will be just as frustrated as you are.

Newspaper

Your local newspaper can also be an excellent source of properties to buy. Most papers have both a real estate section and classified ads section that include real estate for sale. There will likely be hundreds of properties for sale at any one time in the newspaper. You will NOT need to call all of these ads.

By the time that you're looking for houses to purchase, you should already have looked at a bunch of houses in your target area. In fact, you should be an EXPERT in your market and be intimately familiar with retail prices. You will only buy properties that can be purchased at a BIG discount.

Knowing your target area and purchasing criteria, you will be able to quickly screen houses in the newspaper. First, you have determined a target area. Skip over all houses that are not in your area. You can also eliminate houses that are not in your target price range. For example, if you know that you are looking for 3 bedroom (3br) houses that have a market value of $50,000, then using our 70% rule, we need to find 3 bedroom houses that cost no more than $35,000. Of course, not all ads will have the asking price and you might be able to buy some houses cheaper than they are advertised. But in this instance, you could eliminate all houses advertised for more than $50,000.

1 MINUTE TO RENTAL PROPERTY RICHES

To get houses at a big discount, you typically need to find owners that are desperate to sell. Sellers can become desperate for a variety of reasons, including:

- Loss of a job
- Death in the family
- The owner bought another house and can't afford 2 mortgage payments
- Divorce
- The owner wants badly to buy something else, like a boat
- The owner is a bank with too many defaulted loans (REOs)
- Foreclosure

Keeping these desperate sellers in mind, here are some key phrases that you can look for in an ad to indicate that the seller is desperate to sell their house:

- MUST SELL
- Corporate Owner - usually means that the property is a REO
- Handyman's Special - can mean that the property needs a lot of work and therefore may be offered at a discount
- Out of Town Owner - can mean that the previous owner has already moved and therefore has 2 mortgages
- Price Reduced for Quick Sale
- Illness Forces Sale
- Estate Sale
- Auction
- Lost Job
- Foreclosure
- Owner Financing

These are just a few of the key words and phrases you can look for. Can you think of more key words that indicate the seller may be desperate? If so, add them to your personal list!

Drive Your Target Area

Another method of locating properties is to simply drive through your target area and look for houses for sale. You are looking for houses with windows boarded up; with high grass; with lots of sale circulars on the porch, etc. Anything that says they are vacant or distressed. As your rental portfolio grows, this will occur naturally because you will be driving to and from your properties. Simply keep your eyes open for potential deals and you will find them. Taking a different route each day as you drive will also increase you chances of finding a deal.

1 MINUTE TO RENTAL PROPERTY RICHES

Place an Ad of Your Own

In addition to looking at the ads of houses for sale, you could place your own ad. A small classified can be put in most newspapers at a relatively small monthly cost. Some 'penny saver' type papers will even allow you to place ads for free. These ads don't have to be big or wordy to be effective. Here is an ad that I have run with quite a bit of success:

Facing Foreclosure? Need Cash Quickly?
We Buy Houses! XXX-XXXX

If you are placing this ad in the classified ads, you will need to decide which heading to put it under. I like to place it in the "Houses for Sale" section, even though I'm actually offering to buy a house. My reasoning is that people who are thinking of listing their house for sale will look in the "Houses for Sale" section to see what other houses are selling for. Obviously, you could also place your ad in the "Houses Wanted" section. You might even want to try placing it in the Houses for Rent section. Why would you place an offer to buy houses in the "Houses for Rent section"? The answer is that there are often disgruntled landlords with rental properties that they would rather sell than rent again. You could even try all of these sections. Try one for a month, and then another, and another. See which section gets you the most calls or simply rotate on a month by month basis.

If you are going to use this method, it is a good idea to keep an ad in the paper continuously. People will become familiar with your ad and when they decide to sell, they will think of you. However, your ad must still be in the paper when they are ready to sell. That could be months after you first put your ad in the paper.

REIA (Real Estate Investors Association)

Your local REIA can be an excellent source of properties to purchase. There are always new faces at each REIA meeting and many of these people will be new landlords. Often these new landlords will quickly discover that they don't have the stomach for dealing with tenants. These landlords are a perfect example of a desperate seller. In fact, many times a disgruntled landlord will do ANYTHING to get rid of their nightmare. I have had disgruntled landlords give me their buildings subject to their existing financing and I even had one bring cash to the closing.

In addition to disgruntled landlords, serious investors will frequently have surplus deals that they don't want to do. Often, your fellow investors will give you leads on these deals for free. In other instances, these investors will have deals that they will wholesale to you. They make a little money and you still get a great rental.

Auctions

Auctions can be another source of great deals. Auctions can be a little more complicated than a more traditional sale and you need to fully understand what the rules and laws are concerning auctions in your area. Since auctions typically last only a few minutes, you should definitely look at the property in advance of the auction. In addition, you should do some preliminary checking of the title before the auction. You can usually do this yourself on the computer. I would suggest getting a book on this subject and becoming an expert in this field if you are going to pursue auctions. If you intend to bid on a property, be sure that you read the auctioneer's contract. Pay special attention to the payment terms. Finally, DETERMINE YOUR MAXIMUM BID BEFORE THE AUCTION AND DO NOT EXCEED IT! It is easy to get caught up in the bidding and pay far too much for the property!

Foreclosures and Sheriff Sales

Foreclosures and Sheriff Sales are a more difficult way of purchasing properties. You will find these sales listed in the legal section of the newspaper and often on a county website. I do not recommend these sales for new investors. Here are some of the reasons:

- The laws can be complex with these sales
- There can be a redemption period where the previous owner can get the property back even after you've purchased it and rehabbed it!
- It is often impossible to inspect the property before the sale
- It can be tricky to determine if there will be any liens on the property after you buy it
- There can be a criminal penalty if you don't close on the property on time
- The sale can be vacated by a judge under certain circumstances

You should be getting the idea that there is no room for error if you purchase at these types of sales. You MUST become an expert in the laws that apply and you must be thoroughly familiar with the procedures. These can be excellent sources of properties once you have some experience. However, they are not for beginners!

ENTITY STRUCTURING

If you plan on making your rental properties a serious business or even a career, then it is important that you consider entity structuring. Let's assume that your business plan calls for you to accumulate 50 rentals. If you buy these properties in your own name, you will become a big target for lawsuits. Your name will be on all the deeds and all the mortgages. Anyone can find out exactly what you own. Many people in our society dream of getting rich by winning a big lawsuit. Who better to sue than a rich landlord?

As an alternative to this gloomy scenario, you could start one or more Limited Liability Companies (LLCs) to own the properties. The companies would own the properties and you would manage them. Your name would not appear on the deeds and you are not the legal owner. If you are going to own 50 properties, then you might want to start 5 companies and have each company own 10 properties. Then, even if one company is sued and found liable, you would not lose everything and maybe not anything at all!

I am not a lawyer, nor do I play one in books or on the internet. Therefore, I am not giving you advice, legal or otherwise. My suggestion is that you consult a smart lawyer who specializes in asset protection for real estate investors. Even better, you could do some research; read a book; or complete a course on asset protection.

You will want to explore the different types of entities and the different strategies for asset protection. You will also need to thoroughly understand your state laws.

In most states, the Limited Liability Company (LLC) is generally considered the preferred entity for holding rental properties. Land Trusts can be used in conjunction with LLCs to provide both privacy and liability protection, making it VERY difficult for anyone to find out who actually owns the property.

Regardless of how you choose to hold your rental properties, you definitely still need insurance. Insurance is a key part of a multi-layered defense strategy to protect you from lawsuits. In such a strategy, a Land Trust could provide the privacy, the LLC would provide the liability protection, and the insurance would be the last line of defense. The more difficult you make it for someone to successfully sue you, the greater the likelihood that no one will try.

PURCHASING TECHNIQUES

There are many different ways to purchase rental properties. The simplest is for the buyer to simply write a check for the property and the seller to transfer the deed (Of course, the buyer should have a title search done and obtain title insurance before the deal is closed). Unfortunately, most of us do not have an unlimited supply of cash. For the majority of Americans, even if we only had to put $5,000 of our own money into each deal, we could not do many deals. If we are to make a living operating residential rentals, it normally requires that we own quite a few properties. Therefore, we need some techniques that will preserve our cash and still allow us to buy a large enough number of rentals that we can make a nice living.

Even if we are not going to put a lot of our own money into purchasing the rentals, it is still necessary that we have a reserve of cash or credit to cover all contingencies. In my experience, you are at the greatest risk when you only have a few rentals. That is because vacancies and unusually large expenses (like a lawsuit or severe damage done by a tenant) have a greater impact on your total cash flow when you only have a limited number of rentals and thus a limited cash flow. As your portfolio grows, you are less affected by any single unexpected expense.

Pay Cash and Refinance

One of the easiest ways to purchase a property is to simply pay cash. If you have a significant amount of cash, you might want to consider this method. There are many advantages to paying with cash.

- You can often get a better price if you can pay cash, sometimes a much better price. The reason for getting a better price is that the seller knows the deal should close and knows that they are not at the mercy of the buyer's bank granting them a loan.
- Paying cash also means that you can close quickly. This is also a powerful tool that can get you a lower price. In our instant world, many people want to sell NOW. If you can satisfy that desire, they are often willing to take a significantly lower price.
- Buying with cash means that you can start receiving rent sooner. By closing quickly, you can get the property rented and therefore increase your monthly income sooner.
- Paying with cash will elevate your stature as an investor. When sellers know that you're a serious investor, you will get more deals! Likewise, when people know that you are serious, people will begin to **call you** with deals! Instead of spending your time hunting deals, the deals will come to you!!!

1 MINUTE TO RENTAL PROPERTY RICHES

Of course, most of us can not afford to pay cash for a lot of rentals. We might be able to pay cash for one property, but only one. The key here is to get your cash back as quickly as possible. To do this, simply arrange with the bank to refinance the property soon after you've bought it. I strongly suggest that you use a small local bank for your mortgage needs. Small local banks are often more willing to work with investors than big national banks or mortgage brokers. In addition, if you use a mortgage broker, you will pay an extra fee because they are simply a middle man.

"Seasoning" can become an issue with refinancing a property that you've just bought. Seasoning is a term that refers to how long the property has been owned before you sell it or refinance it. Although seasoning is a much bigger problem when selling a newly acquired property, this issue could creep into a refinance also. Always ask your bank about seasoning at the beginning of the refinance process.

While we're talking about banks, it is very important that you get to personally know the players at the bank or banks that you'll be using. Banking is all about relationships. Get to know the president or vice-president if possible. You can meet a lot of important people in your town by joining civic organizations. Get involved!

CAUTION: If you followed the suggestions in this book and bought the property at a big discount, it may be possible to get additional cash back at closing. Many of the gurus promote this in their courses. Do NOT borrow more money than is needed. Remember, you will be repaying the loan with interest. A higher mortgage payment means a lower cash flow and CASH FLOW IS THE LIFEBLOOD OF YOUR BUSINESS. Many new investors have failed because they had a mortgage payment that was too high.

Borrow the Money

If you don't have the money to pay cash, you can simply borrow the money to buy your properties. Obviously, you will need good (decent) credit if you are going to use this method. Again, I always recommend using a small local bank. If you don't know which bank to use, ask a successful investor at your local REIA. The successful investors at your REIA will know which banks are investor friendly. If you get to know these successful investors, one of them may even introduce you to the bank's president or vice-president.

1 MINUTE TO RENTAL PROPERTY RICHES

If you use this method, I recommend going to the bank with a "Funding Request" packet. You should put this packet together before your first meeting at the bank. The packet should include:

- A cover letter discussing what you want to do, i.e. buy an investment property and borrow $xx,xxx from the bank.
- Current Portfolio - list all current property that you own with appraised value, loan balance, current equity, and cash flow (for investment properties).
- Business Plan
- Personal Financial Statement
- Cash Flow Analysis - for the rental properties that you already own. In addition, you might want to include a projected Cash Flow Analysis for the property that you are trying to have financed.
- Current Mortgages - list the current mortgage loans that you have and their current balances.
- Insurance - provide the Declarations Page for insurance policies that you currently have on real estate.
- Appraisals - provide the most recent appraisals that you have for property that you currently own. Do not waste money on an appraisal for the property that you want to buy. The bank will do this and they will want to use THEIR appraiser.
- Deeds - include copy of deeds for properties that you already own and a copy of the deed for the property that you intend to buy.
- Leases - include copies of the leases for rental properties that you currently own and for the property that you intend to buy, if the property is already rented.
- Tax Returns - include copies of your last 2 years tax returns
- Credit Report - include a current copy of your credit report, if you have one. The bank will do one of their own, but it is nice to provide one upfront.

Put all this information in a high quality three ring binder. I like to use the type that has pockets on the front and spine so that you can include a customized cover on them. I have included an example of a binder cover and spine cover page in the appendix of this book.

Other People's Money (OPM) or Other People's Credit (OPC)

The next few topics will cover techniques that can be used to purchase properties with Other People's Money (OPM) or Other People's Credit (OPC). These techniques allow you to purchase property without using any of your own money. While this sounds great on the surface, there are many negative aspects to these types of deals that must be considered. I will present both the positive and negative aspects of these techniques in this book.

As with everything in real estate investing, it is important to be thoroughly educated on these techniques before you use them. Entire books have been dedicated to many of these techniques and they often require special forms and paperwork. In addition, there are state laws that govern these techniques in many states. Always be sure that you understand the laws of your state before trying to buy properties using any of these techniques.

This book contains a basic overview of using OPM and OPC. This is NOT a comprehensive discussion of these subjects. I would strongly urge you to continue your education by reading some good books on the specific techniques that interest you.

Owner Financing

This is very simple! The seller owns the property free and clear. You buy the property from the seller and the seller finances the property for you. In this situation, the seller is acting just like a bank would. At the closing, you will get the deed to the property and the seller will get a note/mortgage promising to repay the seller's loan. If you don't pay, the seller can foreclose and retake possession of the property.

In my experience, you won't find too many of these deals. The number of people who own their property free and clear is very small and the number of those that are willing to sell with owner financing is even smaller.

Owner financed deals can be excellent when you do find them. Often, you can get a very good interest rate and won't be required to have a down payment. In addition, because you're not dealing with a bank, you will save almost all of the closing costs. Obviously, you should still do a title search and get title insurance.

1 MINUTE TO RENTAL PROPERTY RICHES

Subject to the Existing Financing (Sub to or Sub 2)

This is where we really get creative. A "Subject to" deal is one in which the buyer takes the seller's property and simply begins making the seller's payments for them. This is not a loan assumption as they generally have not been allowed for many years. In this sub 2 scenario, at closing the seller transfers the deed into the buyer's name, but the seller's existing financing stays in place. The buyer makes the loan payments for the seller.

Obviously, this is a quite risky for the seller. The seller is trusting the buyer to make the loan payments and pay the insurance. The seller no longer owns the property since the deed has been transferred, but the loan is still in the seller's name. If the buyer does not make the loan payments, the SELLER would be foreclosed on! If the buyer doesn't pay the insurance and the place burns down, the seller would still legally owe the balance of the mortgage (although the seller would probably sue the buyer). I would NOT sell a property Subject 2 because of these risks. However, I have bought several properties this way.

How do you find these deals and why would anyone in their right mind sell a property subject to the existing financing? DESPERATION! A truly desperate seller will do ANYTHING to get rid of their property - including selling it Sub 2. The properties I have bought this way were from desperate landlords who absolutely hated dealing with tenants. They couldn't eat or sleep at night. For them, being a landlord was like living a nightmare! They just wanted out!

The advantages of buying a property Sub 2 are many.

- The buyer does not need to apply for financing.
- The buyer gets the deed at closing and legally owns the property.
- The seller still has the mortgage and is legally obligated for it.
- Closing costs are very low. The buyer should have a title search done and get title insurance.

There is one downside to doing a Sub 2 deal. Almost all loans have a "Due On Sale" clause. This clause can be used by the bank to call the loan due in full if the property is sold. Therefore, when the deed is transferred, the bank can enforce this clause if they wish to. Normally, this does not happen. As long as someone makes the payments, the bank will never know that the property has been sold and usually won't care even if they do find out. You should just be aware that this could occur. If the bank did call the loan due, the buyer would need to obtain a loan in order to keep the property.

Entire books have been written on Subject 2 deals. If you intend to do this type of deal, it would be worth becoming an expert on this technique before you do your first Sub 2 deal.

© 2006 Ciara International, Inc. - All Rights Reserved   www.1minutetorentalpropertyriches.com

1 MINUTE TO RENTAL PROPERTY RICHES

Lease Options

This is yet another no money technique. When you "buy" a property using a lease option, you are actually renting (leasing) the property and you have an option to buy the property. This is a good technique when you have gotten too many loans recently at the bank and need to wait a little while before applying for another. Another situation where a lease option can come in handy is when you want to try out a property for a period of time before actually buying it. For example, you might want to try investing in apartment buildings after doing a few single family houses. You have heard that the tenants in apartment buildings are much harder to work with and that the vacancy rate is higher. You decide that you want to try the apartment building for a year before actually buying it. A lease option is the perfect way to accomplish that.

To buy a property with a lease option, you will sign two documents. The first is a standard lease, although the lease can be for an extended period of time like 2, 3, or 5 years. The second document is the option. An option gives you the right, but not the obligation, to buy the property for a certain price and for a defined period of time. Theoretically, the Lessor (person leasing you the property and granting the option) MUST sell if you exercise your option. Normally, the Lessee (person leasing the property and buying the option) will pay something for the option. This could be $1 or $10,000, whatever the Lessee and Lessor agree to.

Where would you find a seller that would be willing to do a lease option? Once again, the answer is a "desperate" seller. However, in this case we have a seller that is a little more educated. The seller may realize how risky it is to sell via a Sub 2 deal and therefore won't sell it to you Sub 2.

There is another situation that might suggest using a lease option. Suppose that you find a desperate seller in your home town. The seller banks at the same bank that you do. In this instance, you would not want to do a Sub 2 deal, as it might appear to your bank that you are trying to do something sneaky. Therefore, you could either go to the bank and get a loan for the property or do a lease option.

It is important to note that with any technique, including both the Sub 2 and Lease Option, you MUST still buy at a discount. Also, keep in mind that if you fail to exercise your option to buy the property, all improvements that you made during the term of your lease will belong to the owner.

Entire books have been written on lease option deals. If you intend to do this type of deal, it would be worth becoming an expert in the subject before you do your first one.

Selling with a Lease Option

In addition to buying a property with a lease option, it is also possible to "sell" a property with a lease option. You'll notice that I said "sell", but in reality you are renting (leasing) the property and granting the renter the option of buying the property for a certain period of time and at a certain price.

The theory behind "selling" a property on a lease option is that you can:

- get higher than market rents.
- charge a non-refundable option premium.
- get a higher than normal sale price.
- get the tenant to do all maintenance.
- get the tenant to pay the insurance.
- get the tenant to pay the taxes.
- get better tenants that will take better care of the property.

Sounds great, doesn't it? But why in the world would a tenant (buyer) do this?

- You are "selling" the property to a person with bad credit who can not get a conventional mortgage.
- The purchase price is fixed for the term of the lease and option. Since properties tend to appreciate in value, the "buyer" is hoping that the house will appreciate during the term of the lease, thereby giving them equity.
- The "buyer" ties up the house for a period of time while they are working on their credit.
- The "buyer" may get a rent credit from the "seller". The rent credit is a portion of the rent that applies toward the purchase price and is negotiated between the parties. The amount of this credit can be anything that is agreed to.
- If house prices do not increase or the "buyer" changes their mind for any reason, they are not obligated to buy the house. They simply do not exercise their option.
- The "buyer" feels that doing a lease option is better than throwing money away on rent, even though in fact, they are renters.

Okay, so we've talked about the theory. But now let's discuss the reality.

1 MINUTE TO RENTAL PROPERTY RICHES

The Reality of Selling with a Lease Option

Theory is not always reality, and lease options are a perfect example of that. Here are some of the realities of "selling" a property using a lease option.

- Higher Rents - it sounds great that you could get higher rents for a lease option property than for a normal rental. However, the rent associated with lease option deals is often not much more than regular rent and this is offset by the rent credit that the "seller" usually gives to the "buyer". The rent credit is a portion of the rent that is credited to the purchase.

- Option Premium - one of the reasons often given for "selling" with lease options is that the owner can get a non-refundable option premium. This option premium is a fee for granting the option and the gurus suggest getting an option premium of somewhere between $1,000 and 10% of the purchase price. Even more impressive is that this option premium is received in addition to the normal security deposit.

    This does sound appealing and in fact is possible. I have done these myself. However, things are not quite as rosy as they seem. The truth is that the vast majority of renters do not have enough money to put down a security deposit AND a significant option premium. Make no mistake, these people are RENTING your property and almost by definition, they don't have a lot of money. If they did have some money and decent credit, they would be buying a house, not doing a much more expensive lease option.

    While you are waiting for that rare person to appear who has a bunch of money (for the rent, security deposit, and option premium) but terrible credit, your house is sitting vacant. All this time, you are still paying the mortgage payment on the property AND are losing the rent that you would have gotten if you had simply rented the property. If the property sits vacant very long, you will actually lose money by waiting for a lease option "buyer".

- Maintenance - many lease option contracts require the tenant to do all the maintenance. This sounds great because maintenance is a significant expense with rental properties. Unfortunately, the reality is that the lease option tenant often does not have the money or skills to do the maintenance, or simply does not do it. Then, when they do not exercise their option to buy your property, you get a property back that is in terrible condition and requires a lot of expensive maintenance.

1 MINUTE TO RENTAL PROPERTY RICHES

- Insurance - BE CAREFUL WITH THIS ONE! Many lease option "sellers" have the "buyer" be responsible for the insurance. If you are going to do this, IT IS CRITICALLY IMPORTANT THAT YOU HAVE THE TENANT GIVE YOU THE MONEY FOR THE INSURANCE AND THAT YOU PAY THE INSURANCE DIRECTLY. If you don't do it this way, the tenant may stop paying the insurance. If the house then burns down before you discover that the insurance has been cancelled, YOU will have lost your property and it won't be covered by insurance. Could you sue the tenant in this case? Yes, but it will be difficult or impossible to collect!

    NEVER trust a tenant to do anything. Always remain in control!

- Taxes - BE CAREFUL WITH THIS ONE ALSO! This is exactly the same issue as the insurance. If you are going to make the tenant responsible for the taxes, IT IS CRITICALLY IMPORTANT THAT YOU HAVE THE TENANT GIVE YOU THE MONEY FOR THE TAXES AND THAT YOU PAY THE TAXES DIRECTLY. If you don't do it this way, the tenant may stop paying the taxes. If the tax bills are being sent to the property, you may not realize that the taxes have not been paid until the government has put a lien on the property and your property is headed to a tax sale!

    NEVER trust a tenant to do anything. Always remain in control!

- Better Tenants - one of the reasons often given for selling with lease options is that you will get a better class of tenant. The theory is that the tenant will be buying the property and therefore has an interest in taking care of the property.

    The truth is that the majority of lease option "buyers" do not exercise their option to buy the property. The reality is that they were always just renters and that they may always be renters. They have made bad choices in their life. They can't hold a job. They have very little money and bad credit. In addition, they would not take care of a house even if they did own it.

    Moreover, once they come to the decision that they don't want to stay, they may become angry that you won't give them back their non-refundable option premium. At this point, they may decide to severely damage your property just to 'get even'.

    Hopefully, you now understand that "selling" a property using a lease option is no panacea. In fact, it may not be as profitable as simply renting the property to a normal tenant!

1 MINUTE TO RENTAL PROPERTY RICHES

Sandwich Lease Option

A Sandwich Lease Option is a special type of lease option where you buy a property using a lease option and then sell the property on a lease option. In theory, here is how it works.

You find a person willing to sell you their property on a lease option. Let's say that the seller is willing to lease it to you for 2 years at $500 per month and give you an option to purchase it at a price of $50,000. You agree and give the seller $1,000 as an option premium, You are now controlling this property for the next 2 years and can purchase it at any time for $50,000.

Being a shrewd investor, you now find someone who wants to buy this property from you on a lease option at a higher lease payment; at a higher price; and with a higher option premium than you've paid. In our example, let's say that the buyer you find will pay you $600 per month in rent; give you $2,000 for the option premium; and agrees to pay you $60,000 when he exercises his option.

So, how did you do in our theoretical example? You made $1,000 on the option premium (you paid $1,000, but received $2,000). You made a $100 net cash flow on the rent (you paid $500 per month and are receiving $600 in rent). You will make $10,000 IF the "buyer" exercises his option. WOW! Why wouldn't you just do lease options everyday? It sounds great!!!

Before you get too excited, go back and read the previous section entitled "The Reality of Selling with a Lease Option". Every one of those issues is pertinent to Sandwich Leases. In addition, there is one other significant risk that you should be aware of.

Here's the scenario. You've "bought" a property using a lease option. Keep in mind that when you "buy" using a lease option, you are actually leasing the property and have an Option to buy it. You then "sell" the same property to someone else with a lease option. Both leases are for 2 years. After about a year, your "buyer" sends you a written "exercise of option" letter, telling you that he is ready to buy the property. GREAT! You are selling this property to your buyer for $10,000 more than you are paying for it! Anyway, back to reality. You immediately send an "exercise of option" letter to the person that you are buying the property from. The next day, you get a call from the owner who says that he has changed his mind and no longer wants to sell! Obviously, you have a written contract and he can't do that! He says "SUE ME"! You call your "buyer" and tell them that you can't sell the property to them. YOUR BUYER SUES YOU! In the period of only 2 days, you went from thinking that you were a real estate genius to getting yourself into two lawsuits! What do you think of sandwich leases now? This is the main reason that I never do them!

1 MINUTE TO RENTAL PROPERTY RICHES

Purchase Procedure

Regardless of which technique you use to purchase a property, there a few things that must be done for every purchase. The following is a list of tasks that are normally accomplished during each purchase:

- Obtain Financing - <u>it is critical to identify sources of financing before you even start looking for deals</u>. Small local banks are often the best choice for investors. Talk to other successful investors in your area and ask them which banks they use. The investor might even introduce you to a bank officer. Talk to a decision-maker at the bank if possible. The bank president, vice-president, or chief loan officer can make things happen and often are not required to ask a loan committee for a decision. Discuss your plans and get pre-approved.

  Many of the best deals depend on the ability to close quickly. That is exactly why we need to obtain financing before we start looking for deals. Great deals often occur because the seller is DESPERATE and needs to sell NOW. If you do not have cash or at least proof of financing (a pre-approval letter), you will often not be able to take advantage of these deals. The seller will simply look for a buyer that has cash or has been pre-approved.

- Purchase Contract - After you find a property that you wish to purchase, you need to make a written offer using a Real Estate Purchase Contract. This contract is included in the appendix of this book. Once both parties sign the contract, it is a legally binding agreement.

- Perform any inspections that were agreed to in your purchase contract. Examples would be a termite inspection, mold inspection, whole house inspection, etc.

- Back to the Bank - now that you have a signed purchase contract, go back to the bank with your funding request. The loan process needs to be started quickly because it typically takes at least 30 days from loan application to closing.

- Title Search - whether you are obtaining a bank loan or using a no-money down technique to purchase the property, it is very important to have a title search done. The title search ensures that the seller actually has clear title to the property and is able to legally sell it! An attorney, bank, title company, or escrow agent can usually do the title search for you. If you are financing the property via a bank loan, the bank will almost certainly have this done as part of their loan and you will not need to duplicate that.

1 MINUTE TO RENTAL PROPERTY RICHES

- Title Insurance - I strongly suggest that you obtain title insurance for your new property. Title insurance will protect you from lawsuits in the event that a title issue arises later.

- Survey - a survey is expensive and you should decide if you need or want one. The survey identifies the boundaries of your property and ensures that your building(s) are not encroaching on your neighbor.

- Review the Settlement Statement, also called the HUD Statement, the day BEFORE the closing. The settlement statement contains all of the numbers associated with the deal. It identifies exactly how the money is to be distributed and which expenses each party is paying. I have frequently found mistakes in the settlement statement and have been able to save money by having these mistakes corrected. Finding any mistakes the day before the closing will allow the numbers to be corrected before the closing. Discovering mistakes at the closing will normally delay the closing.

- Get a certified check for any funds that you need to take to the closing. You will get the amount from the Settlement Statement when you review it. If you are unable to get a copy of the Settlement Statement before the closing, the closing agent (bank, title company, lawyer, etc) will be able to give you the amount.

- Closing - after everything is done, you will go to the "closing". At the closing, all documents will be signed; the seller will receive his money; and you will receive the deed. It is important to ensure that the deed is recorded at your county's recorder's office.

- Keys and Deed - before leaving the closing, be sure to get the keys, garage door openers, and the deed. Depending on the situation, the closing agent may keep the original deed and record it for you or you may need to record the deed yourself. Either way, be sure that the deed gets recorded.

That's it, you are now the proud owner of a rental property!

REHABBING RENTALS

If you are going to be in the rental property business, you WILL be involved with rehabbing! This is true even if you buy properties that are in perfect condition. The reason:

TENANTS!

Owning a rental property is nothing like owning a personal residence. My family and I have lived in the same house for more than a decade. We raised two children and have a dog. The carpet still looks new; there are no holes in the walls; the paint looks great; and the wood floors shine like the day the house was new. We take care of our house and are proud of where we live.

Contrast that to the typical rental property. The carpet might last 2 years. Rentals need to be painted about every other tenant. Tenants frequently put holes in the walls. Tenants frequently attract roaches and mice due to their unsanitary lifestyles. Their pets chew the woodwork and put holes in the carpet. Their children write on the walls. In other words, TENANTS ARE HARD ON RENTAL PROPERTY!

Rehabbing a rental property is much different than renovating your personal residence or even rehabbing a house that is to be sold. Operating rental property is all about making money. One of the biggest mistakes that new landlords make is to rehab their rental property like they were going to live in it.

One of the first rental properties that I bought was an older two story house. It was an absolute mess. Every door was broken. Every wall had many holes in it. Many of the windows were broken. The house had been a crack house and I bought it very cheap because the landlord had been mentally and financially broken by the tenants. I was a brand new landlord and had yet to be educated about tenants. I was determined to make the house a masterpiece!

My father, my wife, and I spent an entire month working on that house. FIFTEEN THOUSAND DOLLARS in materials along with our labor did indeed turn the old house into a masterpiece. We put in all new windows; all new doors; an entirely new kitchen including all new cabinets and appliances; track lighting; beautiful crown molding in nearly every room; an entirely new laundry room; and beautiful berber carpet. It was magnificent!

1 MINUTE TO RENTAL PROPERTY RICHES

Fast forward three years and four tenants. My latest tenant has just moved out. As I opened the front door, literally fifty cockroaches fall off the inside of the door. Roaches cover the carpet, walls, and ceiling. I have never seen so many roaches. There literally must be ten thousand of the little black creatures in my 2-bedroom house! As I walk through the house to inspect the damage, several roaches fall from the ceiling and strike me on the head. One even slides down inside my shirt. It is enough to make even a seasoned landlord sick!

There is a rip in the living room carpet that runs the entire length of the room. The tenant has painted the walls in an effort to cover up her children's artwork. Unfortunately, she got more paint on the beautiful hand-stained woodwork and the carpet than the walls. Two of my beautifully hand-stained solid wood doors were torn from the hinges. Every single one of the new windows was missing its screen. The carpet was so dirty that it looked like it was 20 years old. Nearly every light bulb in the house was missing. The trap was disconnected under the new kitchen sink and evidently had been for some time. Water has caused the bottom of the brand new cabinet to collapse. There is also a soft spot in the floor near this cabinet.

I could go on and on, but you get the idea. THIS IS A TRUE STORY! It happened to me and similar things (and worse) have happened to every serious landlord that I know. Welcome to the real world of landlording and rehabbing.

What did you learn from this true story?

Here are a few of the lessons to be learned about rehabbing rental properties.

- Consider Your Tenants! If you are rehabbing a vacation property on Martha's Vineyard that caters to wealthy tenants, then by all means do a first class rehab. Marble countertops; stainless steel appliances; and hand-stained crown molding are definitely appropriate and necessary. However, if your rental property houses low income tenants in the inner city, then you should rehab accordingly. Spending time and money on marble countertops; stainless steel appliances; and crown molding is ridiculous with this class of tenant. For me, this was a lesson learned the hard way. In fact, I have to laugh at myself every time I think of putting crown molding in my lower middle class rental property. How stupid and naïve I was!

- Do Not Do More Than Necessary! Considering your tenants, don't spend one dime more than is necessary to make your rental safe, sanitary, and appropriate for the class of tenant. Remember, we are in business to make money. Every penny needlessly spent on a rehab is another penny of lost profit!

1 MINUTE TO RENTAL PROPERTY RICHES

- Do the Work Yourself. You can save a lot of money by doing the rehab work yourself. Much of this work is very simple, yet labor intensive - like painting, cleaning, patching holes in the walls, and replacing light bulbs. All of this work can be learned. Everything that you do will save you money. When I first started in this business, I had never done any rehab work. Today, I do everything except heating and air conditioning. I learned many of these tasks from a home improvement book that I purchased at Lowes.

Here are some specific rehab tips:

- When possible, paint the old wood floors in low income rentals. Low income tenants can destroy carpet in under a year. If they want carpet, then let them buy throw rugs.

- Install used appliances in low and middle income rentals. You can buy used appliances that look good and are about 1/3 the price of new. I buy these used appliances both from used appliance stores and from individuals advertising in the newspaper.

- Paint all of your rentals the same color - off white. Buy your paint at Wal-mart and paint everything this color. Do not use a different color for trim. Off white is a neutral color that the vast majority of people will like and it looks clean. By always using the same color, you can easily touch up spots when needed.

- Do Not Replace Old Cabinets. If your rental has old cabinets, you can often repaint them instead of replacing them. I always paint them gloss white.

- Use Cheap Carpet. There will be occasions when you need to install carpet. This can occur because the floors in your low income apartments are not suitable to be painted. It may also be necessary to install carpet in middle income rentals for competitive purposes. I always buy the cheapest carpet possible. As I said earlier, tenants can and do destroy carpet quickly. It does not matter whether you put in an expensive carpet or a cheap carpet, you'll be lucky if the carpet lasts two years.

- Carpet in Bathrooms and Kitchens. Carefully consider the flooring that you will put in bathrooms and kitchens. I have tried everything and found that there is not a good solution. Tenants typically destroy vinyl floors in a very short period of time. Wood flooring can be easily damaged by water. I have found that putting commercial carpet in kitchens and bathrooms of low and middle income rentals is the best solution. We do not install padding under the carpet in kitchens and bathrooms, because the pad retains moisture.

LANDLORDING BASICS

Many people find landlording to be the most challenging thing they have ever done! In fact, it can be so "challenging" that the majority of new landlords quit a short time after they start. If the truth was to be told, "shocking" might be a better word than "challenging". The best way to turn this shocking experience into a positive one is to be properly educated in the basics of being a landlord. Let's start at the beginning.

Finding Tenants

Once you have a rental property and have it ready for occupancy, the very first thing you need to do is find a tenant. There are many ways to find tenants including:

Newspaper Ads

Putting a small ad in the classified ad section of your local newspaper is probably the most popular way to advertise your rental property. Before placing your ad, carefully look to see how the ads are arranged. Are they arranged alphabetically? Are they arranged by the date the ad was placed, i.e. the longest running ad is at the top? YOUR AD NEEDS TO BE THE FIRST ONE!

In my local newspaper, they arrange the ads alphabetically. Here is my ad:

> **Beautiful 1, 2, 3, 4, & 5 bedroom apartments and houses. We accept Section 8. We love pets! Call XXX-XXXX**

You'll notice that I started my ad with the word "Beautiful". This is good enough to put my ad in the top spot in my newspaper. If I needed the letter "A" to make the top of the list, I'd change my ad to:

> **Absolutely Beautiful 1, 2, 3, 4, & 5 bedroom apartments and houses. We accept Section 8. We love pets! Call XXX-XXXX**

1 MINUTE TO RENTAL PROPERTY RICHES

Yard Sign

Another excellent way to advertise your property is to put out a yard sign or put a sign in the window. I prefer the yard sign because it is more visible. You can buy these cheaply at any home improvement store. I strongly suggest putting a telephone number on the sign <u>that will be answered by a person</u>. Many callers will hang up if they get voice mail. In this business, the person who answers the phone is often the winner.

Internet Sites

There are many internet sites available to advertise your rental property. Personally, I would not spend much money on these. The majority of tenants will find you either through the newspaper or a "For Rent" sign. My local newspaper includes a free internet ad when you place a classified ad.

Word of Mouth

Never underestimate the power of personal connections. Tell everyone you know that you are a landlord. You'll get many leads from this 'word of mouth' advertising.

Other Tenants

Once you become established in the rental business, you can use your existing tenants as a source of new tenant applicants. We offer our tenants a $50 cash referral fee for every person they refer that actually moves into one of our rentals. Many of our tenants work hard to find new tenants for us. At $50, this is a bargain and we only pay when we get a new tenant!

Section 8

Section 8 is a government program that provides housing assistance to low income tenants. These programs are administered through the local HUD housing office. If you will accept Section 8, then you can get on the housing provider list at this office and also may post an ad on their bulletin board. This is absolutely free and can be another excellent source of leads.

1 MINUTE TO RENTAL PROPERTY RICHES

Screening Tenants

Once you get your advertising out there, the phone will begin to ring. I receive an average of 30 to 40 calls per day from potential tenants. With this volume of calls, it is imperative that you have a plan for dealing with these people.

Phone Screening

I learned early in my career that you can not meet every person that calls. It simply takes too much time. The vast majority of callers are not possible tenants for one reason or another. In fact, I often wonder why many of them call at all. The best answer I can devise is that a lot of renters are FICKLE. That's why they are renters. Many of them go from job to job (if they work at all). They make poor choices. They don't plan beyond today. They often don't even know what they want when they call. You probably think I'm joking, but this is absolutely the truth. They often don't know what they're looking for.

With all these issues, it is critical that we pre-screen the callers while they are on the phone. With 30 to 40 calls per day, it is also important that we learn to keep the calls short. My goal with every call is to keep it under 1 minute. The key is to keep the caller focused; get the info I need; do an initial screening; and get them off the phone. To accomplish this, I follow the same pattern with each call:

- Determine what they want. How many bedrooms? Are they looking for an apartment or house? Are they looking for a certain location?

- Tell them what we have available. Give them the address, rent, security deposit, and a few highlights about each rental.

- Tell them about the $25 non-refundable application fee and initial screening criteria.
    We will NOT accept tenants:
    - that have had an eviction in the past 5 years
    - that have had their utilities shut off within the past year
    - that have had a felony in the past 5 years
    - that have had more than 2 misdemeanors in the past 5 years
    - that have any record of drug activity in the past 5 years

- Ask them if they have any pets. Explain the pet policy, additional rent, and additional security deposit for pets.

- Tell them to drive by the property. If they like it, call us back and we'll be happy to show them the inside.

- End the call

Pet Policy

Since I brought up the matter of pets, let's take a minute to discuss the subject of pets in rentals.

Many, if not most, landlords do not allow pets in their rentals - PERIOD! This is because they believe that pets are destructive, noisy, dirty, smelly, unsanitary, dangerous, and a general nuisance. All these things can be true and you may not want to accept pets either.

However, I do accept pets and I use them as both a marketing tool and an additional source of income.

As I already said, most landlords do not accept pets. In fact, they are so adamant about this issue that they put "NO PETS" in their newspaper ads. This creates a market niche for the landlord that is willing to accept pets. It will increase the number of potential tenants for you and keep your vacancies lower. It also gives you a valuable marketing tool. Just putting "We Accept Pets" or "We Love Pets" in your advertising will get your phone ringing!

Pets are a money maker. We charge $25 extra rent per month and an extra $100 security deposit for one cat or one SMALL dog. We charge $50 extra rent per month and an extra $200 security deposit for a medium or large dog. Obviously, you could charge anything that you want (if your customers will pay it, of course).

CAUTION: Do not accept vicious dogs under any circumstances. Check with your insurance company and check your local and state laws to determine which breeds are considered vicious dogs.

Included in the appendix is a copy of our Pet Addendum. Fill it out each time you have a tenant with a pet.

1 MINUTE TO RENTAL PROPERTY RICHES

The goal of the phone screening is to quickly eliminate the callers that won't make suitable tenants. Simply asking the tenant how many bedrooms and what location they are looking for will eliminate many applicants. Obviously, if we don't have what they want, they will not be interested. This step can be accomplished with your newspaper ad if you are advertising an individual rental. Just put the address and number of bedrooms in your ad. If they are not interested, they won't even call.

Definitely tell the applicant the rent and security deposit on the first call. Many callers do not have enough money for the rent and security deposit and will be eliminated. DO NOT "WORK WITH" TENANTS ON EITHER THE RENT OR SECURITY DEPOSIT! They either have it in full before move-in or you won't take them!

If the applicant has not been eliminated and is still on the phone, tell them about your non-refundable application fee and your basic screening criteria:

> We will NOT accept tenants:
> - that have had an eviction in the past 5 years
> - that have had their utilities shut off within the past year
> - that have had a felony in the past 5 years
> - that have had more than 2 misdemeanors in the past 5 years
> - that have any record of drug activity in the past 5 years

THIS WILL ELIMINATE A LOT OF CALLERS. In my experience, about 75% of callers for low income rentals can not pass this criteria. Do NOT negotiate with callers. These criteria are set in stone!

Finally, tell them to drive by the property and call you back if they are interested. Then, get off of the phone as quickly as possible.

If you follow this procedure, you will have eliminated the majority of callers from consideration. This may seem contrary to our goal of renting the property, but it is not. Screening the tenants on the phone simply eliminates the unacceptable callers at an early stage and saves you time and money. In addition, we DO NOT want to meet with criminals, drug addicts, felons, and other unacceptable people. By eliminating them during the first phone call, we have eliminated the need to meet these people in person!

The Second Call

A few of the callers that you talked to will actually drive by your rentals and then call you back. Now you have a possible tenant. During the second call, they will want to schedule an appointment to see the house. Pick a time that works for both of you and schedule the appointment. If your appointment is not in the next hour or so, then I tell the applicant to call me 30 minutes before the appointment to confirm that they are still coming. If they need an appointment on another day, then I just ask them to call on that day.

REGARDLESS OF THE DAY OR TIME OF THE APPOINTMENT, THE TENANT MUST CALL ME 1/2 HOUR BEFORE THE APPOINTMENT OR I DON'T GO TO THE PROPERTY! This is a key point! Tenants are Fickle! Did I already mention that? A million different things can come up to change their plans. Tenants are notorious for not calling to cancel, even if you ask them to. Failing to have the tenant call to confirm your appointment will result in a lot of wasted time sitting at the property waiting for no-shows. Before I instituted this policy, I had almost a 50% no-show rate. After instituting this policy, no-shows are almost non-existent!

Finally, remind the tenant to bring their application fee with them to the showing. This will save you a second trip to the property.

The Showing

The moment has finally arrived to meet the prospective tenant. There are a few things that you should do prior to their arrival to ensure that the showing is successful.

- SAFETY! Safety should be your number one concern! There are a lot of people out there who are criminals, sex offenders, drug addicts, and other wackos. The majority of these dangerous people are renters and you will be coming into contact with them on a regular basis. Take some steps to protect yourself. Here are a few ideas.

  - Take a friend or family member to the showing. Don't show the property alone if there is an alternative.
  - Consider protection. Many landlords carry a concealed handgun. If you don't feel comfortable with a handgun, you might consider mace.
  - Always carry your cell phone.
  - Park so you can get out. Don't park where the applicant can block you in.
  - Tell someone where you'll be.
  - Turn on all the lights in the rental.
  - Meet during daylight hours.

1 MINUTE TO RENTAL PROPERTY RICHES

- **Remove All Tools and Valuables**

It is important that you remove all tools, equipment, and any valuables that you had in the property prior to showing it. The property should be exactly as the tenants will receive it. The purpose of removing your tools and belongings is to reduce the risk that your property will be the target of a robbery.

As you get into this business, you will be shocked at the number of rental property applicants that are criminals. It is common to check the background of an applicant and find out that he has a multi-page criminal history. These people can take advantage of the opportunity of looking at your property to see if there is anything worth stealing.

- **Turn on All Lights**

Realtors use this technique when showing houses for sale. A well-lit house is much more attractive than a darker one. Simply turning the lights on will get you additional tenants!

Visual Screening

During your initial meeting with the applicants, you should begin evaluating them. I start with their car. Is the inside littered with trash, beer cans, and uneaten food? Are the tires bald? Is the exhaust loud? What does all this mean? If the inside is dirty, cluttered, and half-eaten food is all over, then you should expect your property to look like this if the tenant moves in. If the tires are bald and the exhaust loud, it could mean that the applicants don't have enough money to repair their car. This is a warning sign that they may have trouble paying the rent.

Also, look at the people. Do they look normal? Is their manner normal? Do you smell alcohol or marijuana on their breath? Do they have tattoos on inappropriate areas, like their head, neck, and hands? Do they have a tongue ring or other unusual piercings that are visible? Are they wearing any gang clothing or have gang tattoos? Are their pants so baggy that it takes one hand to keep them from falling down? People act and dress like they are. If they look like a hoodlum, they probably ARE a hoodlum! Trust your instincts.

Ask them where they are living now and why they are leaving. Tenants that complain about their current landlord are often troublemakers! Obviously, some tenants do have bad landlords, so again, trust your instincts.

1 MINUTE TO RENTAL PROPERTY RICHES

Taking the Application (and their Application Fee)

After the showing, if the potential tenant desires to rent the property, then they will need to fill out the application. The application that I use is included in the appendix to this book. Before I give them the application form, I again cover our criteria with them and collect their $25 application fee. It is important that they fill out all sections of the application. Particularly important is that they include the first name, last name, middle initial, social security number, and date of birth for EVERYONE that will be living in the rental. We need this information so that we can do the credit check and criminal background check. After the applicant is finished with the application, ask to see their driver's license. An applicant without a driver's license is cause for concern. It usually means that they have been either been convicted of driving while intoxicated or they are hiding something. Applicants have been known to put someone else's information on the application to get past the credit check and criminal background check. Always be sure that the picture on the driver's license is the applicant and that the information on the application matches the license! WHEN DEALING WITH APPLICANTS, NEVER ACCEPT ANYTHING AT FACE VALUE! You can not even believe that they are who they claim to be!

At the same time you are doing the criminal background check, you should check for any civil suits that the applicants have been involved in. Have they been sued by anyone? Have they sued anyone? Have they sued several people??? If so, that certainly sets off alarm bells for me! The very last thing I want is a tenant who is trying to get rich suing people. Landlords are a popular enough target without picking a tenant with a track record of being sue happy!

Criminal Background Check

In my opinion, the criminal background check is the most important part of your screening check. CRIMINALS ARE DUMB! It is difficult for them to stay out of trouble and they will usually have a criminal record. I always start my screening of a potential tenant with the criminal background check. You can often do this check for free on the computer by checking with your county's common please court and your city's municipal court (or whatever the courts are called in your area). If you have any reason to believe that the applicant has spent time out of your area, then a nationwide search should be done. You can do a nationwide search by using almost any screening service. Ask at your local REIA to see who the local investors use or do an internet search under "tenant screening services".

During the criminal background check, you will also discover any evictions that the applicant has had. Never accept anyone that has had a recent eviction. In my opinion, this is an automatic disqualification! NO EXCUSES!

Credit Check

Tenant credit reports can be checked instantly on the internet. Again, ask at your local REIA to see who the local investors use or do an internet search under "tenant screening services". Remember that most tenants will have poor credit. If they had good credit, they would own a house. More important than a credit score is their credit history. Is their credit bad because of unpaid bills from several years ago or is their credit bad because of recent events? I am much more concerned when I see recent problems on their credit report.

Employment Check

Not every tenant will have employment. Many tenants make a career of living on public assistance. For those that are employed, check their employment history. A work history of two months at one fast food restaurant followed by an month at another does not constitute a suitable work history. It is important to verify that the phone number they gave you for their employer is valid. I do this by looking up the phone number for the employer myself. Without doing this, you will often be speaking to a friend of the applicant who is pretending to be their employer. Remember, DO NOT TRUST ANYTHING THAT IS ON THE APPLICATION! Verify everything!

For tenants who do not work, you still need to verify their income. This may be from social security, welfare, alimony, etc.

A good rule of thumb for income is that the tenant should make three times the rent. This is necessary so that the tenant will have enough money not only for the rent, but for the utilities, fuel, food, and other necessities.

If the tenant does not have enough income or their credit report is bad, then you can have one of their relatives with good credit be a co-signer. Be sure to do a credit check and criminal background check on the co-signer. A lease addendum to include the co-signer is included in the appendix.

Previous Landlord Check

You will want to check with the applicant's previous landlords to see what kind of tenants they were. The landlord where the applicant currently resides may or may not tell you the truth about the applicant. If the applicant has been a nightmare, the landlord may say ANYTHING to get rid of them. This may include telling you that they are model tenants when in fact the opposite is true. For that reason, it is important to check with the landlord of the tenants' prior residence. This landlord has no reason to lie about the tenants and will normally give you a much more accurate opinion of their behavior.

I do not trust anything that an applicant puts on the application. Therefore, instead of calling the phone number that the tenant lists for their current and previous landlord, I look up the tenant's address on the county auditor's website and find out who the owner is. This owner should be the same person that the tenant listed as the landlord. Then, I look up the owner in the phone book to see if this number matches the phone number given by the tenant. Doing your screening this way only takes a few extra minutes, but it can really shed some light on any attempted scam by the applicant. Unfortunately, these scams occur far too often. A little detective work by the landlord goes a long way toward ensuring that you get a good tenant.

1 MINUTE TO RENTAL PROPERTY RICHES

Be the Manager, Not the Owner

As a landlord, you must choose who you want to be. No, I'm not suggesting that landlords are schizophrenic or have an identity crisis. What I am suggesting is that you should give some serious thought to whether you are going to represent yourself to the tenants as the manager or the owner of the property.

We live in a litigious society. Many lower class people believe that their dream life is only a lawsuit away. Combine that with the myriad of predatory lawyers out there who make their living sucking the money from anyone with a few assets. I have been the target of these low life predators and have seen the mentality and greed of both the envious and their lawyers. We fought the predators for a full two years and spent $15,000 in legal fees; but we did WIN! Others have not been so fortunate!

The reality in our country is that you do not need to do anything wrong to be sued. ABSOLUTELY NOTHING! All that is necessary is for someone to want what you have and to make a claim or commit a fraud. Then, one day you wake up and you are the target of a lawsuit. Generally, the goal of the plaintiff and the lawyer is to extort a quick settlement. After all, if you're being sued for half a million dollars, you might feel that spending $50,000 to make it go away is a good deal. This kind of defendant mentality is exactly what these predatory lawyers are counting on.

Now back to our decision. Do you think that you would be a bigger target for these predators if you are a lowly property manager or a rich property owner? Be aware that it doesn't really matter if you are rich or not, the only thing that matters is whether you APPEAR to be rich. To someone who is living on public assistance because they are lazy, almost every middle class person would appear to be rich! The lawyer is usually a little smarter than the plaintiff, and they will judge the lawsuit by the assets they perceive the defendant to have. If they check the public records and find that you own 10, 20, 30, or 50 rental properties, you will become a prime target for a lawsuit.

So, what choice do you have? After all, you want to own rental properties! I suggest that you do NOT own anything (or at least as little as possible) in your personal name. Buy your properties through LLCs (Limited Liability Companies) or other entities. The LLC is the legal owner - NOT YOU! NEVER TELL ANYONE THAT YOU OWN PROPERTIES, ESPECIALLY THE TENANTS! Advertising the idea that you are the owner simply makes you a target for lawsuits! DO NOT DO IT! Is this lying? ABSOLUTELY NOT! If your properties were bought in an LLC or other entity YOU ARE NOT THE LEGAL OWNER! If you don't believe me, call the county auditor and ask who owns the property in an LLC. The auditor will tell you the LLC owns the property.

1 MINUTE TO RENTAL PROPERTY RICHES

So, if you are not the owner, what are you? YOU ARE THE MANAGER! Again, this is legally correct. You are the manager of the LLC and their properties. You are an employee of the company, just like any other employee.

There are many benefits to conducting your rental property business this way. As we've already mentioned, the tenants will be much less likely to sue if they think a company owns the property. Tenants often perceive a company as a big, impersonal monster that would be difficult to fight. While they might sue YOU if they think that you own a bunch of properties, they often will not sue that big monster!

In addition, if your properties are divided into different LLCs, a lawyer looking at the owner will likely not find out how many properties you truly own. For example, let's say that you own 50 properties. You have these 50 properties divided into 10 completely separate LLCs. When the lawyer looks up the owner of the property, he will discover that a LLC owns the property. He will then do a search on this LLC and discover that the LLC owns 5 properties. Suing someone with 5 properties may or may not be worth his time. Even if he did discover that you "own" 45 other properties in 9 other LLCs, it will be very difficult for the lawyer to get at the properties in those LLCs. The L's in LLC stand for Limited Liability and the legal intent is that a lawsuit against one LLC will not affect other property that you have in other LLCs. In addition, even if someone wins a lawsuit against your LLC, it is very difficult for them to collect. Check with a good asset protection lawyer for more information.

Another very good reason to "be the manager" is that you will have far fewer arguments with the tenants. The tenants can understand that you work for a big mean company and that you have no choice but to enforce the company's regulations. They will understand that you must collect the rent on time or evict them. After all, employees who don't follow the rules get fired and they know that you don't want to get fired. Contrast this to someone who "is the owner". If you own the rental property, then the tenant knows that you have the ability to bend the rules. In fact, they know that the owner can change the rules or ignore the rules altogether. If you are the owner, the tenants will constantly badger you for this or that. Can they pay the rent late? Can they have new carpet? Can they have five of their best friends move in? It never ends!

The bottom line is that you want to be the manager. Do not tell ANY of your tenants that you are the owner.

Here's another little tip. Do NOT drive an expensive vehicle to the rentals - EVER! Nothing says to the tenants that you are rich and deserve to be sued, like driving up in your Mercedes or Corvette. Either drive a pickup or other work type vehicle, or buy an old junker to take to your rentals. A little common sense goes a long way to staying out of lawsuits.

Privacy

I strongly suggest that you use a cell phone for all of your business activities, especially dealing with the tenants. There are good reasons to use a cell phone:

- You can answer your phone wherever you are. Many applicants for rentals will hang up if they get an answering machine. In addition, there are times when it is advantageous for the tenants to be able to reach you right away. An example might be when a water line breaks and you need to get there to shut the water off.

- If the tenant has your cell phone, they won't be calling your home number. In fact, I strongly recommend that you have an unlisted home phone number. As a landlord, you will be evicting people and they tend to be angry when they are suddenly homeless.

- You can store all of your frequently called numbers, including your tenants, in your cell phone. It is very handy to have all of your real estate contacts with you wherever you are.

It is also very important to use a Post Office Box for all of your business correspondence.

- Again, privacy is an issue. You certainly do not want your tenants to have your home address. I know a landlord that had an angry tenant show up at her home. The tenant blocked the driveway and would not leave (or allow the landlord to leave). This could have been a very dangerous situation. NEVER give the tenants your home address.

- If you own your properties in entities, such as LLC's, you should keep your business address separate from you home address. There are many reasons for doing so, but one of the main ones is to prove to the IRS and the courts that your company really is separate from you. When a company has its own checkbook and its own address, that is significant proof that the company really is a legitimate business.

1 MINUTE TO RENTAL PROPERTY RICHES

Prior to Move-In

Now that you've thoroughly screened the applicants and chosen your new tenant, you must ensure that everything is done properly prior to giving the keys to your new tenant. I've included my "Real Estate Leasing Checklist" and copies of all the forms that I use in the appendix to this book.

Lease

The lease MUST be signed by the tenant before you allow them to move in. This includes any lease addendums that are appropriate including the Co-Signer Form, Pet Addendum, Property Modification Agreement, and Paint Addendum. These forms are all included in the appendix and you should thoroughly understand them before you sign up your first tenant.

It is important to take a few minutes to explain the lease to the tenants. I cover the entire lease and all its provisions so that there will be no misunderstandings later. I also emphasize when the rent is due and that we do not accept any excuses for late rent. IF THE RENT IS NOT PAID ON TIME, WE START THE EVICTION PROCESS IMMEDIATELY!

While we're on the subject of leases, let's discuss a little philosophy about the term (length) of the lease.

First, it is important to point out that a lease is a contract. It is legally binding on both parties. However, a contract is not worth anything if it can not be enforced. With lower income rentals, we really have no way of enforcing the contract.

For example, let's say that you have one nice house that rents for $1,000 per month and one low income house that rents for $350 per month. The nice house is rented by a young couple that is just starting out. They recently graduated from college and they both work full time jobs. They are renting your house while they are saving money for their dream house. Your other rental is being rented by a young single mother that gets nearly all of her money from government assistance. She is a third generation welfare recipient and dropped out of high school when she got pregnant for the first time at the age of 15.

Our young college graduates have every reason to follow the lease. They are upwardly mobile and want to build their credit. An eviction is absolutely the last thing that they want on their record. If they did default on their lease, we could sue them and we could collect. They both have jobs and income that could be garnished. We can enforce this lease.

1 MINUTE TO RENTAL PROPERTY RICHES

The young single welfare mother is quite another case. She is a high school dropout. She is not upwardly mobile and has a very bleak future. In fact, this woman will probably live her entire life on public assistance. If she defaults on the lease, we can sue her but we will not collect. Her government assistance can not be attached by any judgment. We have virtually no way to enforce this lease, other than evicting her.

Now let's turn these situations around. We are the "rich" landlords. We not only have a bright future but our present is pretty good. We have assets (rental properties) and we have income (rental income). The tenants and their lawyers know this. Our low income tenants can even get a free lawyer through the local Legal Aid office. In short, the tenants can always enforce the lease against us. If we violate the lease, they can sue us and they will collect from us.

The point of this discussion is that a lease is only meaningful when it can be enforced. We should take this into consideration when we decide on the length of a lease that we sign with our tenants.

I would suggest that you should sign a one year lease in your nicer single family home rentals. Since you can enforce the lease against these tenants, by signing a one year lease, you will virtually assure that your property will be rented for at least the next year. You are locking the tenant in for that period of time and they are not likely to violate the lease.

<u>I would also suggest that you should only sign month-to-month leases with your low income tenants.</u> To do otherwise is pointless. Since you can not realistically expect to enforce a lease on low income tenants, signing a one-year lease ONLY benefits the tenant!

Cosigner Form

This form should be completed when you are requiring the tenant to have a co-signer on the lease. We do this when we believe that the tenant is a risk but the tenant has a relative or friend who has excellent credit; has a good job; and has some assets (like a house). In these cases, we have the relative or friend sign this form which makes them responsible for the rent and damages to the house if the tenant fails to pay.

If you are going to use a co-signer, it is very important that you do a background check on the co-signer, just as you do for the tenant.

1 MINUTE TO RENTAL PROPERTY RICHES

Pet Addendum

In an earlier chapter, we discussed the advantages of accepting pets in your rentals. If you decide that you will accept pets, you should complete this form each time that you accept a tenant who has a pet. This forms details the rules concerning pets and gives you recourse if the rules are not followed. As with all forms and contracts, the tenant must sign it.

Property Modification Agreement

Tenants often want to modify or alter your rental property and volunteer to do the work themselves. In almost every case where I have permitted this, there has been a problem. Remember - No Good Deed Goes Unpunished! I have learned this lesson the hard way on many occasions.

There are many problems that can occur when tenants are allowed to work on your property:

- The work is often substandard and will need to be redone at your expense later.

- The tenant starts the work and never finishes it.

- The tenant removes the improvement when he leaves and your property is damaged.

- The tenant could get hurt while doing the work and then sues you!

- The tenant could claim that they were an employee and that you didn't pay them or provide benefits to them. This could land you in trouble with the state's labor department and worker's comp.

- The tenant often expects to take their labor out of the rent, even if you've specifically told them that you will not pay them.

I strongly advise you NOT to let tenants do improvements or modifications to your property. If the tenants want something done, either you should do it yourself and have them pay for it, or have it done by a professional at their expense.

If you do decide to let tenants improve, alter, or modify your rental property, then fill out and have them sign the property modification agreement.

1 MINUTE TO RENTAL PROPERTY RICHES

Paint Addendum

If you want to experience a landlord nightmare for yourself, let a tenant paint! I made this mistake several times when I was a new landlord. In every case, the tenant did a TERRIBLE job, often getting more paint on the carpet than on the walls. When it comes to painting, "JUST SAY NO"!

If you do decide to allow a tenant to do some painting, fill out the paint addendum and have the tenant sign it.

Move-In/Move-Out Form

Next to the lease, the Move-in/Move-Out Form is probably the most important document that will be signed by the tenant. This form is use to document the condition of the house before the tenant moves in. This is extremely important as it can be used in court later to prove the extent of damage done by the tenant. In addition to filling out this form and having the tenant sign it prior to move in, it is an equally good idea to take pictures of the property. I keep a cheap digital camera in my truck at all times. It frequently comes in handy in the rental business.

Emergency Notification Form

This form actually serves two purposes. First, as the name suggests, it can be used to contact the tenant's next of kin in the event of an emergency. Tenants frequently get themselves into trouble of one kind or another, and you may need to contact a relative if the tenant is sick, injured, or sent to jail. In addition to using this information for emergencies, the tenant will often put truthful information on this form that they will not put on the application. This information can be used to help track down the tenant if they skip out on the lease.

1 MINUTE TO RENTAL PROPERTY RICHES

Lead Paint Disclosure Form and Lead Paint Pamphlet

The law requires that landlords give each tenant a lead paint disclosure form and a pamphlet regarding lead paint. In addition, the landlord must keep a signed copy of the lead paint disclosure form in his/her records. (see the appendix for these forms)

While we're on this subject, let's talk about lead paint. Houses built before 1978 contain lead paint. Lead paint is dangerous if lead dust is inhaled or lead paint chips are eaten. In these pre-1978 houses, every painted surface should be in good condition. Paint should not be cracking or chipping and all lead paint dust should be cleaned up. It is a good idea to repaint all surfaces with modern paints so that the lead based paint is encapsulated. An area especially vulnerable to paint dust are the windows. As the windows move up and down, the rubbing of the windows in the frames create dust. These areas should be cleaned frequently and painted before each new tenant moves in. If you decide to accept Section 8 tenants, lead based paint is a big deal if children under 6 years old will reside in the house. Children under 6 years old are particularly susceptible to the hazardous effects of lead based paint.

Utilities Transferred to Tenant's Name

PRIOR to the tenant moving in, it is extremely important that the applicable utilities are transferred into the tenant's name. Call the utility companies and check this yourself. If the tenants are allowed to move in before the utilities are switched, you may have a big problem. If the tenant does not switch the utilities, you can not shut the utilities off in most cases. Shutting utilities off is against the tenant-landlord laws in most states. Your only alternative may be to evict the tenants and this may take some time, all the while you will not only be losing rent, but paying their utility bills!

BE SURE THAT THE UTILITIES ARE TRANSFERRED INTO THE TENANT'S NAME BEFORE ALLOWING THEM TO MOVE IN!!!

Keys

Once you've successfully completed all the steps in the "Real Estate Leasing Checklist", you can give the tenant the keys to the property. Be sure that you also have a set, so that you can get in to do maintenance and in case of an emergency.

CONGRATULATIONS! At this point, you've now got your first tenant! I know that it seems like a lot to do, but it really is as simple as following the steps in this book. It will get easier each time you do it!

1 MINUTE TO RENTAL PROPERTY RICHES

Collecting the Rent

This is my favorite part of being a landlord and I'm sure that it will be yours also. Most people with jobs dread the first of the month because that's when all the bills are due. As a landlord, I love the 1st of the month because that is when rents are collected.

There are basically two ways to collect the rent: Personally or Remotely.

Collecting Personally

Collecting the rent personally entails meeting the tenant face-to-face at their rental unit and receiving the rent directly from them. There are several advantages to collecting the rent personally:

- you have a better chance of getting the rent on time.
- you can inspect the property when you collect the rent. I do a quick walk-thru safety inspection of every unit every month. This will give you an early alert when problems arise.
- it gives you a chance to talk to the tenant. I always ask if there are any problems and if everything is working correctly. You would be amazed at the number of tenants that won't say anything even though there are serious maintenance problems.
- It lets the tenant know that you are a hands-on landlord and they tend to take better care of the property.

The only disadvantage of collecting the rent in-person is that it takes a little time and some gas for the truck.

This in-person method is the way I do it and the method that I recommend!

Collecting Remotely

Collecting the rent remotely would include having the tenant send you a check or having a direct deposit arrangement with the tenants.

The advantage to this approach is that you don't need to expend any effort to collect the rent.

The disadvantage is that you will have more late and missed payments. Also, you will not be inspecting the property and therefore will have more problems arise without being aware of them. I do not recommend this method.

1 MINUTE TO RENTAL PROPERTY RICHES

Late Fees

My lease states that the rent is due on the 1st of each month; it is late after 5pm on the 4th; and we begin the eviction process immediately thereafter (on the 5th). If the rent is paid after 5pm on the 4th, there is also a $50 late fee. No exceptions! Don't be confused here, the eviction process normally has a legally required notice period (3 day notice, 7 day notice, etc) during which you have to notify the tenant of the pending eviction before you can file the eviction in court. It is during this period from the rent becoming late until the end of the notice period that you will collect the late fee. After you file the eviction in court, do not accept any money (including the late fee). Once you file the eviction in court, it is too late and the tenant must go.

It is absolutely necessary that you follow the lease to the letter. The tenant MUST pay the rent by 5pm on the 4th or they MUST pay the late fee. There are several reasons for this:

- If you don't insist that the rent is paid on time, I guarantee that it will not be! You should expect that late or skipped rent will get to be the norm.
- If you don't insist that the tenants follow the lease on the rent, they won't follow it on any other provision.
- If you allow ANY tenant to pay the rent late, then all of your tenants will feel that they can pay late. All of your tenants must be treated equally or this may be seen as discrimination against a particular tenant or tenants. In addition, you will be setting a precedent that can be used in court against you.
- Tenants talk to each other! If one tenant is allowed to pay the rent late or you waive the late fee, you should expect every other tenant to know about it and use this against you.
- It is unfair and confusing to the tenant for the lease to say one thing and the landlord to do something else.

In summary, INSIST THAT THE LEASE IS FOLLOWED! The rent MUST be paid on time. Anyone paying late rent MUST pay the late fee! The eviction process will begin immediately upon the rent not being paid on time.

Partial Rent

NEVER ACCEPT PARTIAL RENT! When the tenant asks if they can give you half the rent this week and the rest next week, SAY NO! If you accept partial rent, it will probably be impossible to evict the tenant that month. Tenants know this and will use it to their advantage. They will try to string you along and pay the minimum they can get away with. It is an inexcusable mistake for the landlord to ever accept partial rent. DON'T DO IT! Remember, you are just the manager and the company does NOT allow you to accept partial payment!

© 2006 Ciara International, Inc. - All Rights Reserved   www.1minutetorentalpropertyriches.com

1 MINUTE TO RENTAL PROPERTY RICHES

Evictions

Homework time! Laws are constantly changing and each state has a different law as it applies to evictions. Therefore, it is necessary that you do a little work to become informed and stay informed on the current Tenant-Landlord Law and the Eviction Law in your state. You can usually find this information quite easily by entering 'Tenant-Landlord Law' with 'your state name' in an internet search engine. You can also get a lot of good information on these topics from your local REIA members and a local attorney that specializes in evictions.

If you are to be a serious landlord, it is a sad fact that YOU WILL HAVE EVICTIONS. In my business, I have about a 1% eviction rate per month. Nearly all of these tenants are being evicted for non-payment of rent. To date, I have a 100% success rate in court. It is not that I or my attorney are legal geniuses, but rather that the eviction laws are very simple. If you follow the procedures, the eviction should be granted.

Evicting a tenant can be a very traumatic event for a new landlord. The tenant will often try to blame you for making them homeless. It is especially hard when the tenant has young children, or even worse a new baby. Making matters worse is that your friends and family may think that you are a monster for kicking someone out into the street. If all of this isn't hard enough, your religious values may dictate housing the homeless, feeding the hungry, and clothing the needy. It is a true moral dilemma for most new landlords.

The truth should make you feel better. You are NOT responsible for making the tenant homeless. The tenant made the choice to not pay the rent. The tenant made the choice not to work. The tenant made the choice to spend their money on something other than the rent. The tenant made bad choices and they are paying the price for their decisions. **The tenant is SOLELY responsible for being evicted.**

Unfortunately, your very business may depend on how you handle evictions. As I've said many times before, tenants often make bad choices. That is exactly why many of them ARE tenants! They don't have a good work ethic and they don't spend their money wisely. Their priorities are not that of a responsible person.

I do not want to give you the wrong impression. If you've done a proper screening and have gotten tenants according to the guidelines in this book, the vast majority of your tenants should be good people and should not cause you any problems. At any given time, no more than 10% of the tenants are any trouble at all and only about 1% per month need to be evicted. It is this 10% of tenants who are trouble that I am speaking about in this section.

To be successful as a landlord, you must enforce your lease. In fact, your lease is the only thing that keeps your rental business from descending into chaos. I strictly enforce the lease on all points and ensure that the tenants know it.

Eviction for Non-Payment of Rent

When you have a tenant that asks to pay the rent late or refuses to pay the rent, tell them that you are sorry but the company does not permit that. As the property manager, it is your job to collect the rent in full and on time and you do not have the ability to do anything else. If they fail to pay in full by the due date, then you should begin the eviction process by posting whatever legal eviction notice is required by your state. Here in Ohio, we post a '3 Day Notice to Vacate the Premises' on their door. On the 4th business day after the rent is late (at the expiration of the 3 Day Notice), we file the eviction with the court. Please note that each state has its own requirement for giving the tenant notice. This requirement may include placing specific language in the notice and delivering it to the tenant in a specified manner. IT IS IMPERATIVE THAT YOU FOLLOW THE PROCEDURES FOR YOUR STATE <u>EXACTLY</u>. Failure to follow the correct procedures can result in your eviction being thrown out and you will be required to start over. This can result in duplicate court filing fees and additional months of a tenant living in your property without paying. I strongly suggest having an eviction lawyer help you with your first eviction.

There are some benefits to doing an eviction. Obviously, you are getting rid of a bad tenant. However, when you do an eviction you are also setting a good example for the rest of your tenants. A tenant being evicted will be the talk of the neighborhood. If you rapidly evict a tenant who does not pay the rent, the other tenants will learn not to test you. You will therefore improve your rent collections and minimize the number of evictions that you need to do.

Evicting for Lease Violations

There are times when you will need to evict someone for a lease violation other than non-payment of rent. In my world, this happens most often due to illegal activities being conducted on the premises, namely drug trafficking. Whether the cause is drug activity or something else, I would strongly suggest that you try to turn the situation into a non-payment of rent eviction. The reason is that it is very easy and relatively quick to evict a tenant for non-payment. It is generally much more difficult and can be a longer process to evict for anything other than non-payment.

1 MINUTE TO RENTAL PROPERTY RICHES

Let's look at an example. You have a relatively new tenant in one of your houses. You followed the procedures recommended in this book and did a thorough screening of the tenant. The tenant is a 24 year old female, who had no previous evictions and absolutely no criminal history. Shortly after moving in, you became aware that the tenant had a man living with her. Her lease does not permit anyone other than the tenant to live there and you have asked her about it. She claims that the man is her boyfriend and that he is just visiting. She is adamant that the boyfriend does not live there.

One day, a strong storm moved through your town. Luckily, the house was not damaged but a bunch of large limbs from your tree fell into the yard and a couple are laying on the roof. You contact the tenant to inform her that you will be working on the property and cleaning up the limbs.

The next day, you arrive at the property and begin cutting up the limbs. During the first hour that you are at the property, at least 15 different junky looking cars pull up. Very questionable looking people get out of the cars and go into the house. No one stays longer than 3 minutes. As the day goes by, this occurs all day long. Cars pull up and people go into and out of the house. No one stays longer than a few minutes. It is very obvious, you are the proud owner of a drug house!

Something must be done! You knock on the door and tell the tenant that you know what is going on. She says nothing is happening other than friends like to stop by. You talk to a neighbor who says that your tenant is selling marijuana and that many known druggies are frequenting your property.

You call the police and report the situation. The police tell you that they are well aware of the problems with your house. If you don't do something about the situation, your property may be seized! The police suggest that you evict the tenant immediately!

What can you do? What provisions of the lease has the tenant violated? Now you see where our problem is. The tenant IS violating the lease provision against anyone living in the property other than the tenant. The problem is that if you try to evict the tenant for this violation, the tenant will claim in court that the boyfriend is just visiting. Your eviction claim will be laughed out of court. The tenant IS violating the lease provision against illegal activity on the premises. The problem is that the tenant has not been arrested, not to mention convicted of any crime. Again, your eviction claim will be laughed out of court.

So, what can we do……..?

1 MINUTE TO RENTAL PROPERTY RICHES

Trick of the Trade

Fortunately, when your tenant is violating your lease, there is something that you can do. This is especially true if the violation involves criminal activity, particularly drugs. The reason that this works so well with drug addicts and other criminals is that they are STUPID! REALLY STUPID! We can use that to our advantage.

Here is what I do. I make up an eviction notice detailing the illegal activity. I include every thing that I can possibly think of that the tenant has done wrong. The longer the list of trouble, the better. I wait until the rent is due and then take the notice to the tenant. I let the tenant know that I am quite displeased and that we will be evicting them AND contacting the police. This will make them angry, which is good. At this point, I demand that the tenant pay the rent. They ALWAYS refuse! AT THIS POINT, I'VE GOT THEM! Leave the premises and have no further contact with the tenants. Do not accept any rent from this point further. Follow the eviction procedure for non-payment of rent and your problem is solved.

Pay to Leave

In an effort to avoid the expense and hassle of an eviction, many real estate gurus promote the idea that you should pay your non-paying tenants to leave. The idea is that an eviction typically costs several hundred dollars and at least a month or two of lost rent. You can avoid most of this expense by simply paying the tenant some money to leave, typically a few hundred dollars.

On the surface, paying a deadbeat tenant to leave sounds like a good idea. However, following this strategy can result in disaster, as the landlord loses control of the situation. Here are a few of the things that make this 'pay to leave' strategy so dangerous.

- When you pay the first tenant to leave, you have set a precedent. If you pay one tenant to leave, shouldn't every tenant have the right to expect payment when they stop paying rent? If you don't treat the tenants equally, then the tenant not paid to leave could certainly claim that you are discriminating against them.

  Discrimination is a dangerous issue for landlords and is often more subtle than you might think. When discrimination is mentioned, most people think of a white person treating a black person unfairly. This certainly is discrimination, but not the only kind of discrimination. If you pay a white, healthy male tenant to leave and then decide not to pay a white female to leave, you may be accused of discrimination based on the sex of the tenant! If you pay a white, healthy, male tenant to leave and then decide not to pay a white male with an alcohol problem to leave, you might be accused of discrimination based of the disability (alcoholism) of the tenant!

1 MINUTE TO RENTAL PROPERTY RICHES

If you get entangled in a discrimination claim, then you could easily lose many times the money you "saved" by paying a tenant to leave. A discrimination claim could lead to significant legal fees and the imposition of a fine by the government.

- Don't pay your tenants to steal from you. Tenants talk to each other! When you begin paying deadbeat tenants to leave, you are encouraging your other tenants to stop paying rent when they want to leave. The word will quickly spread that you are a weak landlord and every marginal tenant will try to take advantage of you. They know that when the last tenant failed to pay the rent, you paid him. **You are actually paying people to steal from you!**

- Don't allow tenants to stall! If you make an agreement with a tenant to pay them to move, you must accept their word that they will actually move out. Consider for a moment that they gave their word (in the lease) that they would pay the rent on time. They have already broken their word by refusing to pay the rent. You are now accepting the word of a LIAR that they will move out on a certain day. I can almost guarantee that the tenant won't move as agreed. They will ask for a few more days and then another few days. They will be content for this game to go on forever. Before you realize it, you'll have wasted another month and still have a tenant that is not paying rent.

- Another key concept to understand is that a one day delay in filing an eviction can cost you an entire month of lost rent. Eviction courts take cases in the order they are received. Therefore, the first landlords to file their evictions each month will receive the earlier court dates. Due to legal notification requirements, these early filings may not get a court date for two weeks (or longer). If you give a 3-day notice to the tenant on the 5th, and then file with the court on the 8th, you might get a court date on the 22nd (2 weeks later). Assuming that the eviction is granted, it can take up to 10 days (here in Ohio) to actually have the bailiff setout the tenant.

  As you can see from this example, the landlords that file early in the month may be able to get the tenant out before the end of the month. These landlords will have a chance to rent their house or apartment the next month. All of the successful landlords will file very early in the month. As these landlords file, the court dates will fill up. Within only a day or two, enough court dates will be taken that it will be impossible for anyone else filing to get their tenants out by the end of the month. Even the delay of a day or two can result in the late filing landlord having a rental unit empty for another month.

- Finally, paying a tenant to move will mean that they do not have an eviction on their record. Other landlords will suffer with this tenant because you did not do the right thing and EVICT the deadbeat. Evicting deadbeats not only benefits you, but benefits other landlords.

Do Not Discriminate

It is generally illegal to discriminate in connection with rental housing based on race, color, religion, sex, handicap, familial status, or national origin. From a practical standpoint, it is not only illegal, but EXCEEDINGLY STUPID to discriminate for any of these reasons. As the owner of rental properties, we are in business to make money. We are not in business to further our social agenda, whatever it may be. In fact, from a business standpoint, the only color that I care about is GREEN. I am trying to make money and any tenant that will pay the rent on time; not conduct illegal activities at the property; and not tear up the property is fine with me. Again, it is ALL about the money.

More Homework! You need to know your state's current law as it pertains to discrimination. Some states have more restrictive laws and you MUST know this. Again, you should check with your local REIA (Real Estate Investors Association) or a local real estate lawyer for your state's law. You could also do a Google search for your state's discrimination law.

Is all discrimination illegal? NO! In fact, I discriminate legally all the time. I discriminate against criminals. I discriminate against tenants who have been evicted in the past. I discriminate against the way people look (tattoos on the face, multiple face piercings, gang style dress), etc. I discriminate against the lazy. In short, I discriminate against those that are a high risk for being a bad tenant.

Equally important as not discriminating is that you should not try to help or rehabilitate people. You are not a charity and should only do things in conjunction with your rental business for business purposes. There are an infinite number of tenants with sad stories who make a career of taking advantage of naïve landlords. Resist the temptation to be a nice person. Volunteering at church or your favorite charity is a much better way to contribute and will not jeopardize your income. When it comes to rentals, NO GOOD DEED GOES UNPUNISHED! Sad, but true!

LANDLORDING NIGHTMARES - THE TRUE STORY

Here is a chapter that you won't find in most investing books. I've included an entire chapter of true stories about the *joys* of being a landlord. Landlording can be a true nightmare and this is the second most frequent cause (behind lack of cash flow) of new landlords going out of business. The purpose of this chapter is to give you a feel for the things that WILL happen to you as a landlord. You should decide if your temperament will allow you to endure these incidents without losing your health. The stories are absolutely true, but the names have been changed to protect the troublemakers.

So, without further adieu………..

Crazy Daisy

It had been a long two weeks. Nearly every aspect of the apartment needed to be renovated. There were holes in the walls. The carpet was in tatters. The kitchen was filthy. The stove was inoperative. Just about everywhere I looked was the evidence that the last tenant had destroyed the place. There had been claims of illegal activity and the tenant was rumored to still be in jail. The previous landlord had given the tenant notice that she was in default of her lease and the tenant had apparently abandoned her property in the apartment. Clothes, nasty looking furniture, and trash were strewn about the apartment. Many loads to the dump were required to get rid of all the junk. Finally, all of that was behind me. The apartment was done and it looked GREAT!

I get about 40 calls each day. This particular call was exactly like all the others. Daisy saw our ad in the newspaper and she wanted information about our rentals. From the first call, Daisy seemed like an ideal tenant. She was a young, single mother that needed a place to call home. She seemed perfectly normal. She arrived in a late model clean car. Relatively attractive and well dressed. No tattoos or nose rings were visible. She talked intelligently. Section 8 would pay most of her rent and she already had a job. She wanted the apartment. We took her $25 application fee and ran background checks on her. Her record was almost spotless. One small underage drinking violation was on her record, but nothing else. It looked like we had an excellent tenant.

1 MINUTE TO RENTAL PROPERTY RICHES

It was 6 pm and I was having a good day. Every day that you fill a vacancy is a good day, or at least it seems that way. At 6:30, I received a phone call from Daisy. "The apartment is INFESTED with roaches". Those were the first animated words out of Daisy's mouth. I couldn't believe it. "Daisy, try to settle down", I responded. "I have worked every day for the past two weeks in that apartment and haven't seen a single roach". "Well, I saw a roach", replied Daisy. I calmly explained to Daisy that a single roach does not make an infestation and that I would stop by in the morning with some roach traps. Daisy seemed to calm down and agreed that I would meet with her the next morning to put out some roach traps. In my mind, it was certainly possible that there could be a roach. To put it politely, the tenant that lived downstairs was a slovenly pig and was in the process of being evicted!

Everything seemed to be back in order. After dinner, I sat down to relax and watch the news on TV. The phone began to ring and it was once again Daisy on the phone. "The apartment is INFESTED with mice too!" It was clear that Daisy was extremely upset. "I don't think that I can LIVE here!" Again, I tried to calm Daisy. I reminded her that she had just signed a one year lease and that she was obligated to pay the rent during that period. Moving out would NOT change that obligation. Once again, I promised that I would meet her at the apartment the next morning and I assured her that I would do whatever was necessary to eradicate any pests that were present. As the phone call ended, that sinking feeling in my stomach was evidence that my good day was heading south.

Early the next morning, I arrived at Daisy's apartment. Several small cans were on the floor, unmistakable evidence that Daisy had already fumigated the apartment even with other residents in the building! I explained to her that this could be quite dangerous and that she was not to do this again. Once again, I told Daisy that I was very surprised that there were any pests in the apartment. I had just spent two weeks in the apartment and had not seen any roaches; any mice; and not even any mouse droppings. "I think I know where the roaches and mice came from", responded Daisy. "My furniture has been in my grandmother's garage for several months and I saw a mouse come out of the couch".

All of the grief that Daisy had given me the evening before was for something that she caused! In fact, our apartment was now occupied by several mice and some roaches and Daisy was totally responsible. Be that as it may, I assured Daisy that even though she caused the problem, I would do everything possible to get rid of the pests for her. I put out several mouse traps and roach traps and left the property. I was thankful that the fault did not lie with us and that Daisy knew it. Surely, she would be grateful for our help and I fully expected her to be a model tenant.

1 MINUTE TO RENTAL PROPERTY RICHES

It didn't take long to discover that Daisy was not grateful. Within a few days, she was calling me every day to complain that her apartment was infested with roaches and mice. Of course, her apartment was not really infested. It only had a few mice and a few roaches. We were catching and killing them with the traps. This went on for a few weeks. I made several trips to the apartment to fill every little nook and cranny with caulk, so that mice could not get into the apartment. Of course, in reality this was trapping the mice in the apartment. After all, they started in the apartment in her grandmother's furniture. At each visit, I would ask Daisy how we were doing with the mice and roaches. We were making great progress. In fact, on several occasions, she stated that the pests were all gone, only to have them mysteriously reappear on another day. As time went by, I would not find any evidence of roaches or mice on my trips to her apartment. I began to wonder if she was mentally ill.

One day, when I was at the apartment to caulk some cracks to keep out the invisible mice, I noticed white powder all the way around the perimeter of each room. I asked Daisy about the powder and discovered that she poured Borax all around the apartment. I couldn't believe it! She had a young child that was often on the floor. To me, this seemed insane! I demanded that she vacuum up all the Borax and never use it again.

About this time, Daisy decided to report me to everyone she could think of. All of a sudden, I was a slumlord. She called the local HUD office. She called the Health Department. She called the city building department. She complained that her apartment was unfit for habitation. In reality, it was one of the nicest apartments in the city. The local HUD office called to ask what was going on with this tenant. The Health Department called with questions. Fortunately, they both know that I have some of the nicest properties in the city and they both thought that Daisy sounded irrational on the phone. I was not so lucky with the building department. Some official believed Daisy's story and sent me an order to have a licensed professional exterminate the apartment OR THE ENTIRE BUILDING WOULD BE CONDEMNED! Even though the apartment did not need an extermination, I spent $40 to have a professional do the job, just to get the building department out of the picture. I could have appealed the order from the building department and won, but it was quicker and cheaper to just pay the $40 for the extermination.

After the tenant in the apartment below Daisy was evicted, we began rehabbing this apartment. One day I was working on this apartment with a couple of helpers, when a pair of Jehovah's Witnesses made the mistake of stopping by Daisy's apartment. Up until that time, I did not know that one person could string together such a long litany of the "F" word. This clean cut, All-American looking girl, cursed the evangelists like she was possessed by Satan! She followed them down the stairs, screaming obscenities at them the entire time. Only when they were out of the building and well on their way down the street did she finally stop. When Daisy turned around to re-enter the building, she saw us standing there, mouths agape in disbelief. She smiled at us as if nothing had happened and wished us a good morning. That was the day that Daisy got her nickname - CRAZY DAISY!

1 MINUTE TO RENTAL PROPERTY RICHES

To make a long story short, all of this drama settled down for a few months. Daisy remained a thorn in my side. She was just about the most needy tenant that we ever had.

It was the fourth of the month. I gave Daisy a call to arrange picking up the small portion of her rent that she actually paid (the rest was paid by the taxpayers through Section 8). This was the last day to pay rent without it being late, but Daisy always paid on the last day. I could not get Daisy on the phone, so I drove over to the building. The grass needed to be mowed and I planned to knock on her door while I was at the building. As I approached her apartment door, I could hear that the TV was on and I also heard someone talking. I knocked on the door, but no one answered. I knocked harder and announced that it was the landlord. Again, no one answered. I wasn't very happy that the tenant was ducking me, but I decided to go outside and mow the grass. Maybe the tenant would come out while I was working.

I had mowed about half of the yard when Daisy's boyfriend came out. I asked him why he didn't answer the door and he said that he wasn't there, he had come from down the street. I despise liars! I had seen him come from the building and knew that he was lying. We exchanged some words about his lack of character and he left. A little later, I saw Daisy driving down the street. I walked into the street to talk to her. By now, it was nearly 5pm in the afternoon and the rent was about to become late (the rent is late after 5pm on the 4th). "Are you going to pay the rent Daisy"? "Yes, but I have to run into town and cash my check", was her reply. "I'll wait", I responded. Suddenly, just as if a switch had been flipped, Daisy went BERSERK! She began ranting and raving. I explained to her that if she didn't pay the rent, we would start eviction proceedings immediately and that she would likely lose her government assistance. She screamed "who cares, there is NOTHING that you can do to me!" With that, I left.

A few minutes later, I arrived home. Another frustrating day of dealing with Daisy had ended and I was ready for some peace and quiet. I began to wonder what Daisy meant when she said that there was nothing that I could do to her. I certainly COULD evict her. I certainly COULD notify the local housing office and she would lose her assistance. I certainly COULD be a terrible reference for her in the future. I certainly COULD sue her for damages. She had seen me evict other tenants and knew that I would do it. What she said just didn't make sense. Yes, she did act crazy from time to time, but she did have a lot to lose by being evicted. She had never been late on rent before. Something was going on!

I decided to check the court records to see if anything had happened that I wasn't aware of. I grabbed my laptop and pulled up the city's municipal court site. THERE WAS THE ANSWER, RIGHT THERE ON MY COMPUTER! She had been arrested and charged with 7 counts of theft! She evidently believed that she would be sent to jail. She had probably already lost her job. She might even lose her child. That must be it! That explained everything.

1 MINUTE TO RENTAL PROPERTY RICHES

The phone rang. In my mind, I thought that it might be Daisy who had changed her mind and wanted to pay the rent. I couldn't have been more wrong. It was the police. The officer said that Daisy had filed a complaint and that I was being accused of disturbing the peace. I explained to him that this was a low income neighborhood with frequent trouble and that THERE WAS NO PEACE IN THIS NEIGHBORHOOD. Therefore, since there was no peace, I certainly could not be disturbing it. Furthermore, I explained that the city council, mayor, and police were always talking about landlords being responsible for their tenants and that I was being responsible for mine. I politely suggested that the police should stay out of my business and let me take care of my tenants. I also said that if he wanted to arrest me, that would be fine as I was sure that no jury would convict me of anything. Finally, I explained that Daisy had been recently arrested for 7 counts of theft and that she was nothing but trouble as a tenant and a citizen. With that, our conversation and the issue was over.

The very next morning, I wrote a letter to our local housing office. I informed them that the tenant had not paid her portion of the rent and that I would be evicting her. Since I had already received the housing office check for this month, I would be evicting her at the beginning of the next month. I requested that the housing office not send me any further checks for Daisy, as I could not accept them. (In most state, including mine, it is not possible to evict someone in a month when you've taken partial rent and I had already accepted and deposited the housing office check). Daisy was notified by the housing office that she had violated her agreement and that her housing assistance was being terminated. In the only good decision she had made since moving in to our apartment, she moved out voluntarily and I did not need to evict her. To tell the truth, I had mixed feelings about that. It was certainly good that I didn't need to spend hundreds of dollars on the eviction. However, because she was not actually evicted, nothing would appear in her court records and this would make it more likely that another landlord would accept Daisy as a tenant. Someone else would likely be enduring Daisy's crazy behavior because there would be no legal record of an eviction.

My nearly year long association with Crazy Daisy was over. She had been nothing but trouble since the day she moved in. She was finally gone. Good Riddance!

Daisy's story, however, had not quite ended. Daisy finally got her day in court. She was convicted on multiple counts of theft and sentenced to jail. Maybe justice was served after all!

Lessons Learned from Crazy Daisy

I included this true story to give you an indication of the everyday situations that landlords get into. This is the real world of landlording. Frustration is a frequent companion when you're dealing with tenants. They frequently act irrationally and as in this case may even be mentally unbalanced. Even worse, some of them may be taking illegal drugs and they can be dangerous.

Every prospective landlord should look deep inside to decide whether they can live with this kind of stress. Stress, conflict, and frustration are very much a part of this business. Can you sleep at night with these conflicts going on or will being a landlord destroy your well-being?

There were a lot of things that I did right with this tenant. I thoroughly screened her before she was accepted. I made every effort to take care of her, even though she caused the problems. When she failed to pay rent, I immediately followed the law in my state to evict her, and was able to get her out without an expensive eviction.

There was at least one thing that I could have done better. Having a loud argument with the tenant in the street was very unprofessional. I let my frustration with her get the best of me instead of just acting like a professional. This resulted in the police contacting me and could have led to my arrest for disturbing the peace. In the future, I will try to remain more objective, although this is not always easy. You can see that even an experienced landlord can be affected by all the nonsense and stupidity that comes with dealing with tenants.

Chemical Attack

I like to get up early. On most days, I will be up and doing some paperwork by 6 am. I also like to relax and watch the news of the day on television each evening. One evening at about 9:30 pm, my wife and I were watching a cable news program. The tasks of the day had been completed and the phones had stopped ringing. Everything looked good for an uneventful and relaxing night. Then, in the manner that many landlording nightmares start, the phone began to ring. One of my tenants was on the line. "Someone sprayed a chemical into the building and everyone is choking and having trouble breathing". Those were the tenant's exact words. So much for my relaxing evening!

I asked the tenant if she had called the police and the fire department. She said that she would do that as soon as she hung up. I instructed her to get everyone out of the building and to immediately call the police and the fire department from a neighbor's house. I also told her to call me back if she needed me to drive to the building.

1 MINUTE TO RENTAL PROPERTY RICHES

I did not receive any additional calls that evening, so I decided to try to relax and check with the tenants the next day. The next morning, I drove to the apartment building to see how the chemical attack had ended. As soon as I opened the door to the building, I could see the evidence of the attack. A white powder was covering everything in the common areas of the building. I knocked on the door to apartment number 1. The tenant that had called me the night before answered the door. I asked her what the police and fire department said. Apparently, the authorities had decided that someone had opened the front door and fired a chemical fire extinguisher into the common hallway. No one had been injured and the only damage was the white powder that covered everything. I got a mop and bucket of water, and had the common areas cleaned up in half an hour. Not a big deal!

Lessons Learned from the Chemical Attack

In my early days of being a landlord, this would have been a big deal! I'm sure that regardless of the time of night, I would have rushed to the building. However, as my landlording experience has grown, I have become numb to all the drama. Low income tenants have a lot of drama in their lives, and I have learned to not let their drama traumatize my life.

The other lesson to be learned here is that in an emergency, tenants should be encouraged to get safely out of the building first, followed by contacting authorities and only then contacting the landlord. SAFETY FIRST!

No Good Deed Goes Unpunished

Randy called me looking for an apartment. He had a girlfriend and a young child and they needed a place to live. Randy was very upfront about the fact that he had a felony on his record and he presented a convincing story that he had one youthful indiscretion and was trying to put his life back on track. I am not a sympathetic landlord and have absolutely no sympathy for criminals. I have very specific screening criteria and I follow them to the letter.

Although Randy was a convicted felon, his felony conviction had been 6 years earlier. He did not have any criminal record since then. He had no evictions and met all of our other requirements. I decided to take a chance and rent the apartment to him.

It wasn't long before I regretted my decision. About a month after moving in, Randy decided to have a big fight with his live-in girlfriend and the police were called. By the time the police arrived, Randy was so out of control that he had to be tazered. After they finally got him in the police car, he kicked out the police car window. Clearly, this tiger had not changed his stripes!

1 MINUTE TO RENTAL PROPERTY RICHES

Things went downhill from there. There were several little incidents. Randy claimed that his kid was burned on the gas stove. There were complaints about roaches, even though they lived like pigs with uneaten food strewn around the apartment. They wanted carpet put in the apartment. It was always something. They were a nuisance.

Then it happened. One month, I was at the building collecting rents. Randy asked me if he could pay the rent late. I told him no, we do not allow late rent. If the rent was not paid on-time, we would post an eviction notice the next day and there would be a $50 late fee. Randy simply refused to pay the rent.

True to my word, I posted the eviction notice the next morning. Randy began to act up. He made threats that he was going to 'get me'. He made a lot of noise and disturbed the neighbors.

A couple of weeks later, the eviction case was heard in court. He made all kinds of wild accusations as many tenants do. He told the magistrate that he and his baby would be homeless and living in their car. All of the accusations and claims didn't mean a single thing to the magistrate. He had not paid his rent and he was evicted.

The next step was the setout. The "setout" is the process where a court bailiff places the tenant's possessions on the curb and gives possession of the property back to the landlord. The setout was scheduled for a week later. Two days before the setout, I received a message from Randy. He said that his mother had been at the property and that the ceiling had fallen on her. She was in the hospital. He wanted me to call him to discuss the situation. I surmised that it was a ploy to keep from being evicted and I did not return his message. That same evening, the mother who had allegedly been injured called. She wanted to know the name of our insurance company so that she could file a claim. Now I understood that this was an insurance scam, not an attempt to keep the apartment. I also understood that the tenant was making good on his threat to 'get me'. Since this was clearly a scam, I did not return her call. The next morning, I got another message from Randy's mother saying that water had caused the ceiling collapse and that the wall was about to collapse! That got my attention. I didn't believe for one moment that this incident was legitimate. I fully expected to find the ceiling pulled down. However, now I was concerned that the tenant might have intentionally punctured a water line. I drove to the building and met Randy outside. He eagerly invited me into the apartment to see the "damage". To my complete surprise, there was absolutely no water damage - NONE! Their claim about water was a complete lie. I could not believe how stupid they were!

Criminals are not very smart. That is universally true and it was certainly true of Randy. Unfortunately for them, the portion of the ceiling they pulled down was made of what I call hairboard. The ceiling looked like it was plaster, but was actually hairboard. It is EXTREMELY light. This ceiling material could have fallen from 10,000 feet and would still not hurt anyone! Another big mistake for the scammers. I COULD NOT BELIEVE HOW STUPID THEY WERE!

1 MINUTE TO RENTAL PROPERTY RICHES

That same afternoon, the tenant moved out. This was a full day before the setout was to occur. I had no way of knowing that the tenant was gone and therefore I met the court bailiff for the setout the next day. The apartment was a mess. The tenant had painted graffiti on the wall outside the front door. Trash was everywhere. They had not taken any food and had left many of their clothes. The tenant was indeed living in his car and I guess they didn't have room for their belongings. It was at this point that I realized the tenant had stolen the gas heater in the living room. I immediately called the police. Within a few minutes, a police officer arrived at the apartment. Here's where I got a break. The police officer had been a landlord and had experienced these bad incidents with tenants. He didn't like these deadbeat tenants any more than I did. I gave the officer the name of the tenant and a description of the tenant's vehicle.

After the officer left, I did one more thing. I spread the word to the other tenants and neighbors that Randy was being sought by the police. I thought that this would put some pressure on Randy and might put him on the defensive.

The following morning, I received a call from Randy. He was at the police station. As it turns out, he heard on the street that he was wanted and went to the police station to see if he was in trouble. Randy asked me if I would drop the whole thing if he returned the heater, even though he claimed that he did not steal it. I said "ABSOLUTELY NOT"! I was not interested in getting the heater back, I was interested in seeing Randy go to jail. One day later, the heater mysteriously reappeared at the back door of the apartment.

About a week after Randy left, I received a letter from an attorney. Randy's mother wanted our insurance information so that she could make a claim. I turned the letter over to my attorney who suggested that I give them the insurance information. Although this would have been the easiest course of action, I decided to fight this obvious scam. I did a little investigating on my own and asked several people what they knew about Mary (Randy's mother). I quickly discovered that she was a widely disliked woman. She had attempted to sue other people for frivolous reasons. She also was allegedly totally disabled from a previous neck injury and was receiving government money. However, I discovered that she was working at least 2 different places for cash and was probably committing insurance fraud and tax evasion. I gave this information to my attorney who sent a letter to Mary's lawyer. The letter said that we believed that Mary and Randy were attempting to perpetrate an insurance scam. If any lawsuit was to proceed, we would be conducting a full investigation into Mary's disability status and her work and tax status. To date, we have heard nothing further from Mary or her lawyer!

1 MINUTE TO RENTAL PROPERTY RICHES

Lessons Learned

- No good deed goes unpunished! This little saying is very true when it comes to business and especially the rental business. In this case, I accepted a tenant who had a good story but a bad history. He technically met our screening requirements because his felony was more than five years ago. However, this tenant had only been out of prison for 3 years and was on parole. Maybe he was just waiting for his parole to end before restarting his criminal activity. In the future, I will not take felons unless they have been out of prison for 5 years.

- <u>It is better to have a vacant rental unit than one occupied by a bad tenant</u>! This is an extremely important concept. From time to time, every landlord will have multiple vacancies. It is tempting to accept the first person that walks in with money. That is a big mistake. A vacant rental will affect your profits, but one bad tenant could eliminate your entire profit from many, many rentals. That didn't happen in this case, but it could have. What if the tenant had done a more convincing job with their scam and been able to successfully sue me? What if the tenant had destroyed the apartment? These would have been expensive incidents and the financial loss would offset the profits from many other rentals.

- Be a hands-on landlord. I am not friends with my tenants and certainly do not socialize with them. However, I do listen to them and try to know what is going on at our rentals. In this incident with Randy, I was able to put the word out "on the street" through the other tenants that Randy was wanted. This put enough pressure on him that he went to the police station. We got our stolen heater back and this was a factor in stopping their lawsuit.

- Be aggressive with lawsuits! When presented with a potential lawsuit, many people will give in and either offer a settlement or hand over their insurance information. In this case, I took a very aggressive position and did some investigating of the plaintiff. I discovered that she was supposed to be totally disabled and yet was working. I also discovered that she was being paid in cash and I suspect that she wasn't reporting this cash to the IRS. When we confronted the plaintiff's lawyer with this evidence, the lawsuit disappeared.

- Know the eviction laws for your state. This tenant thought that because he had a baby and would be living in a car, that he would be able to get out of the eviction. He made a bunch of silly accusations in court and asked that the eviction be denied because of the baby. I knew the law and therefore knew that none of the tenant's claims would matter in court. In my state, if the tenant does not pay the rent, they get evicted - PERIOD!

1 MINUTE TO RENTAL PROPERTY RICHES

Fire!

This beautiful day started like any other day. The sun was shining. The apartments were just about full. Life was good. Everything was quiet throughout the morning and in fact throughout the entire day.

Just down the street from the apartment building is a mental health clinic and many of the tenants of this building are clients at the clinic. These mental health patients are normally excellent tenants and they are often long term tenants. Quite frankly, I wish we had more of them.

Bob Johnson is the tenant in apartment #5. Bob is a long time tenant in this building and acts as the informal superintendent. The other tenants look up to Bob and frequently go to him when they need help. On this evening, Bob was at home and was tinkering with an old radio that he was trying to repair.

At 10 pm, the grandfather clock in the corner started to chime as it does every hour of the day and night. However, this time the chiming didn't stop with the tenth chime….or did it? Bob could still hear a sound that sounded like a distant chime. Bob stopped tinkering with the radio and walked over to the clock. The clock was silent, but the chiming continued. Bob walked around his apartment to investigate the sound. It clearly wasn't coming from his apartment, it was coming from the upstairs apartment. Finally, Bob realized that the chiming was from the fire alarm in the upstairs apartment. Bob was not alarmed, as it was not that uncommon for an alarm to go off. People sometimes burned their food and set the smoke alarm off. Bob went back to his radio. After a couple of minutes, Bob noticed that the alarm was still sounding. That was a little unusual as most tenants would have already removed the battery at this point. He decided to investigate further. As soon as Bob opened his apartment door, he could see an orange light reflecting off the building across the street. As he walked further into the street, he could hear the crackling above his head. He turned around to see that the apartment directly above him was on fire!

Bob was ex-military and was calm in an emergency. He instantly knew what to do. Bob dialed 911 on his cell phone and at the same time he started knocking on the doors of the other apartments. Everyone got safely out of all of the apartments, except the one that caught fire. The nearest fire station is just down the street and they arrived quickly. When they reached the scene of the fire, they discovered that the mentally ill tenant had poured gasoline all over her couch; set it on fire; and then sat down on it! The fire was quickly put out and the troubled woman survived.

1 MINUTE TO RENTAL PROPERTY RICHES

Lessons Learned from the Fire

This incident actually occurred in one of our buildings, but shortly before we actually purchased it from the previous owner. The incident went just about as well as could be expected. A big part of the success was due to an alert tenant that knew what to do in an emergency. Very little could have been done to prevent this incident. The tenant met the screening requirements for tenants and no-one could have predicted that the woman would attempt suicide in such a bizarre manner.

This incident does illustrate the need for working smoke detectors in every apartment. In addition, it is our policy to have a working fire extinguisher in every apartment.

The Nurse

We had just completed the rehab on a two bedroom house on Walnut Street and were ready to show it to new applicants. After only 3 or 4 calls, a registered nurse named Gayle called and wanted to see the house. I gave her the address and instructed her to drive by and call back if she was interested. She did. We set a time to look at the inside of the house. She liked it. She explained that she had been on worker's comp for a quite a time due to an injury and was just about to get back to work. She filled out an application and gave me the application fee. Her screening was fine except for an eviction just a little over 5 years ago. She met our screening criteria but in my opinion she was still an increased risk. I told her that I would accept her as a tenant but that I would require a deposit of $1,000. That was a big deposit for a $500 per month rental, but she agreed.

She moved in and was a model tenant. For the first few months, the house was spotless and there were absolutely no problems. From time to time, Gayle had a female friend, Lisa, staying with her, but there were still no problems. As time went by, I would see her friend Lisa more often than Gayle and Lisa would pay the rent. I was a little suspicious of this arrangement, but the house looked great and the rent was always paid on time. It is not unusual for tenants to have someone move in with them even though the lease prohibits it. This is almost impossible to prove and therefore I didn't give the tenant a lot of grief over it.

One day I was driving to one of our rentals and listening to the radio. The big news on our local radio station was of a drug bust. They described the incident as being a cooperative effort between the police, the county sheriff, and the drug task force. I always listen to these incidents to see if any of my tenants were involved. As you have probably already guessed, the drug bust was at our rental property that was occupied by Gayle.

1 MINUTE TO RENTAL PROPERTY RICHES

I drove straight to the house to see what had happened. As I turned the corner onto Walnut Street, I saw a rental truck sitting in front of the house. Gayle (the tenant) was no where to be found but her friend Lisa had almost finished cleaning out the entire house. I asked her what had happened. Lisa said that Gayle had moved out a couple of months before. Lisa's boyfriend had moved in with her and was selling crack. The police used a battering ram to open the front door and threw in a concussion grenade. The grenade burned a large spot in the carpet. Crack was found in the house. Lisa, her boyfriend, and another person were arrested and spent the night in jail. All three were bailed out the next morning.

The one good thing about this incident was that everyone moved out of the house without the need to evict them. The bad news was that the house was trashed. Unlike the neat and tidy house that I had seen each month when I picked up the rent, this looked like an entirely different house. The front door had been broken in by the police. There was a large burn spot in the living room carpet from the concussion grenade. The police had pulled down some light fixtures; pulled outlets from the wall; knocked several holes in the walls; and generally done a lot of damage. The place was a DISASTER!

The worst part of this entire incident was that only three days after the raid, the police dropped all charges. The reason - THE SEARCH WARRANT HAD EXPIRED! I could not believe it. The tenants were caught with the drugs; my house was badly damaged; and the charges were dropped!

Lessons Learned

- Be careful who you rent to. In this case, I had screened the tenant and she did meet our criteria. She did have a previous eviction, although it was more than 5 years ago. Maybe I should have looked a little longer to find a better tenant.

- Don't be afraid to require a higher deposit (if allowed in your state). I made the right decision when I required a security deposit that was almost double the normal deposit. Since she had that previous eviction, I realized that she was an increased risk and therefore raised the deposit amount. That was very fortunate, because I kept every penny of it to use for the repairs!

- Be a hands-on landlord. Know what is going on at your property. I am a hands-on landlord and keep a close watch on my properties, but I blew it on this one. If this really were a crack house (and apparently it was), I missed it.

1 MINUTE TO RENTAL PROPERTY RICHES

- Read the police reports in your local newspaper every night. If I had not heard of this drug bust on the radio, it would have been imperative that I saw it in the newspaper. If not, the house would have been sitting there vacant with a broken down front door. Druggies and homeless vagrants would have taken over the house and I would have been lucky if the house didn't burn down. Repairing a couple of thousand dollars worth of damage is a LOT better than rebuilding a house that has burned down.

- Meet the neighbors in the area. I try to meet the homeowners around my rentals and give them a business card. By doing so, they will often call me when bad things are happening. If I had done that in this case, someone would have probably called me about the crack house well before the drug bust occurred. I might have been able to pressure Lisa and her drug dealer boyfriend to leave before my house was badly damaged.

Dog

I love my dog! Doodle is a Yorkshire Terrier and is part of our family. Recognizing my attachment with my dog, I fully understand that tenants can also become attached to their pets and want to keep them in their rental property. For this reason, we do accept most pets in our rentals, but ONLY with prior written permission and only when the tenant takes care of their pet.

Donny and his wife Liz had moved into one of our low-income apartments. From the beginning, they were not good tenants. Their apartment was always a filthy mess and their child was growing up in very unsanitary conditions. Roaches were all over their apartment and they continually complained about them. I am normally sympathetic to complaints of roaches, but there is very little that a landlord can do about roaches when the tenants live like pigs. Uneaten food strewn about and dishes that are never cleaned are an open invitation to roaches. They also had at least one mouse in their apartment, but wouldn't cooperate with putting out the traps (that I supplied) because they said the mouse had become a pet.

After several months in the apartment, Donny called me on the day that the rent was due and told me that the rent would be 2 days late because the transmission on his car went out. He claimed that he spent the rent money on the transmission, but that he would have some more money in two days. I reminded him that as the property manager, I was required to give him a 3 day eviction notice on the following day and that I would be forced to evict him at the end of the 3 day legal eviction notice if he had not paid by that time. I also reminded him that he would be required to pay the $50 late fee..

1 MINUTE TO RENTAL PROPERTY RICHES

True to his word, Donny did pay the rent, including the late fee, on the second day. However, when I was picking up the rent, I discovered that they had just purchased a puppy. I told Liz that we did not permit pets without written permission, an additional deposit, and an agreement to raise the rent. Additionally, even though we accept most pets under those conditions, we do not accept dogs that are on the vicious dog list that is provided by our insurance company. I informed her that the dog they bought was an Akita, which is on the vicious dog list. I told her that either the dog had to go or they would need to move. She said that they had paid $400 for the dog and could not get rid of it. "That is your choice", I said. "If you won't get rid of the dog, then you must be out by the end of the month".

A few minutes after I had this conversation with Liz, her husband Donny called. He was very irate and accused me of harassing Liz on the phone. I explained the situation and Donny threatened me with violence.

To fully appreciate this incident, you would have to see Donny. Donny is one of those people who is not blessed with great stature. In the politically correct world, he would be considered vertically challenged. In my real world of straight talk, he was just plain SHORT. I seriously doubt if Donny is five feet tall and he has a real attitude as a result. He was and is a punk. At any rate, I wasn't too concerned about his threat.

Another interesting thing to note about this incident is that the tenant was at fault here, but the tenant blamed the landlord - me! In fact, the tenants didn't do one thing wrong, they did three things wrong. First, they lied about spending the rent on a transmission! The truth was that they spent the rent money on the dog! Second, they bought a dog which was against their lease and without getting permission. Finally, they bought a dog that was on the vicious dog list.

True to my word, the very next day, I posted a 30-day notice to vacate the premises on the tenant's door. Although they were angry and made more threats, they did move out by the end of the month and the incident was over.

Lessons Learned

- Tenants ALWAYS blame the landlord when they violate the lease. That is why they are tenants. Many tenants make bad choices and don't accept responsibility for their actions.

- Always enforce the lease. You can NOT bluff tenants. Even though their word is often worthless, your word must be as good as gold. When you say something, follow through!

1 MINUTE TO RENTAL PROPERTY RICHES

Inheritance

Receiving an inheritance can be a good thing. For example, if a long lost relative leaves you a million dollars, most people would consider that a good thing. Landlords often receive quite a different kind of inheritance, and many times it is anything but a good thing.

When an investor buys a rental property, often the property will already be occupied by a tenant. In most cases, the new owner is required by law to honor any lease that the tenant has with the landlord. Therefore, when a landlord takes over a rental with a tenant, the landlord is said to have inherited the tenant, because the tenant is passed down from the original owner to the new landlord.

I have inherited many tenants. In many cases, this has been an inheritance that I could have done without! James was just such a tenant. He came as part of a four-unit building that I purchased and he proved to be nothing but trouble. From the first time I met him, I could tell that he was a loser. He was a crack addict, a thief, a manipulator, and a liar. Even with all these issues, I still felt some compassion for him. He was a Vietnam veteran and I have the utmost respect for veterans. He was mildly retarded or at least I was convinced of that. I wanted to help him if I could.

James was on Section 8 and was required to pay a portion of his rent. From the beginning, I questioned whether it was appropriate for him to handle his own affairs. In the past, his sister was his payee, paying all of his bills and handling his money for him. James had taken her to court and some bone-headed judge had given James control of his money. Unfortunately, I learned from the previous landlord that James could not handle money and would frequently blow his money before he paid his bills. On the day that I took over the building, I told James that he would either pay the rent on time or be evicted. James was on Section 8, and being evicted would almost certainly result in his termination from the Section 8 program and his becoming homeless.

For the first two months, James did pay the rent on time. However, the rent being paid on time did not mean that all was well. James was addicted to crack. He frequently brought other crack addicts to his apartment. I warned him that we would not put up with illegal activity at our apartment building and that illegal drugs would not be tolerated. Although I warned him about the drug issue, there was absolutely nothing that I could do about it. I had no evidence of the drug activity and no legal means to evict him. In addition, he had most of a 1 year lease left, so I could not give him notice to leave. I was stuck.

1 MINUTE TO RENTAL PROPERTY RICHES

At the beginning of the third month, I realized that there were going to be problems. I could not reach James to get the rent. On the 3rd, I left a note on his door reminding him to call me about the rent. I did not hear from James, either on the 3rd or the 4th. Per our policy, I posted a 3-day legal notice on his door on the morning of the 5th. The clock was ticking!

I try to be a Christian. I am fully aware that as Christians we are supposed to help our neighbor and I wanted to help James. I am a veteran, and as a veteran I simply could not understand how a fellow veteran could get into such a shape. I just can't fathom how someone could have the discipline to be in the military and then end up as a crack addict.

I decided that the only way I might be able to help would be to get in touch with James' only relative, his sister. I called her and explained the situation. "James is about to be evicted and I would like to help him", I said. "Would you be willing to pay his portion of the rent this month if I could get him to go to rehab?" James' sister had experienced many years of misery due to James and his addiction. James had repeatedly lied to his sister and had stolen money from her. It was so bad that James' sister had been forced to move and James did not even know where she lived; he only had her phone number. We agreed that I would try to get James into rehab and that the sister would cover his portion of the rent while he was in rehab.

I arranged for James to be accepted into the Veteran's Administration Drug Rehab program. I told James that he either had to go to the program or that he would be evicted and almost certainly be homeless. James did not want to go, but I set a deadline of the next morning. The next morning, I arrived at his apartment at the agreed upon time and he was not home. He was avoiding me again. I went back to his apartment later that day unannounced and caught him at home. I gave him an ultimatum - "Go with me NOW to the VA, or I will immediately file for eviction!". Finally he agreed to go.

I helped him gather up a few belongings and drove him to the VA. After an hour or so, the doctor finally came in to evaluate James. I told the doctor that James was addicted to crack and that if he was not admitted into the drug rehab program, I would immediately evict him and he would be homeless. James was admitted to a 30-day rehab program and I felt good about my decision to help. I called James' sister and gave her the good news. Maybe I could make a difference in at least one person's life.

Things went well for the first 14 days. James even called me a few times from the hospital and told me of his progress. He seemed to be doing great and I had high hopes of having a drug-free tenant who could start a new life. It felt wonderful to be able to actually help someone and to make a real difference in his life.

1 MINUTE TO RENTAL PROPERTY RICHES

On day 15, I received a call from James. "I want to come home", James said. "They are making me get up at 6am every morning and I can not do it". I tried to reassure James and encouraged him to stay. He became agitated and insisted that he was going to sign himself out. He did.

Within three days of coming back to the apartment, James was once again hanging around with known drug addicts and bringing them to his apartment. Even worse, he allowed another drug addict to move in with him. I had evicted this drug addict from the building when we took it over. That was the last straw! I called James' sister and told her not to send us any more rent. I also told her that as soon as James missed a rent payment, I would immediately evict him.

I did not have long to wait. At the beginning of the next month, James spent all of his rent money on crack. I notified my local housing (Section 8) office and immediately started the eviction procedure. Within a couple of weeks, we went to court. James was evicted and became homeless. I have seen James on the streets a few times since then, and I believe that he is still homeless to this day. I am hoping that James will finally hit bottom and will get the help that he so desperately needs.

Lessons Learned

- **No Good Deed Goes Unpunished!** Unfortunately, this is very true in business. Every single time that I have tried to help someone, it has backfired! The lesson is that you should conduct your business like a business, and do your charity work through your church!

- Do not allow drug addicts to stay in your rentals. They hang around with other drug addicts and repel good tenants.

- It is extremely difficult for crack and meth addicts to be cured. Take this into consideration when considering anyone with ANY drug history, even if it occurred more than 5 years ago. Failure to find a recent police record does not mean that a drug addict is cured, it only means that they haven't been caught.

- Evict immediately for non-payment of rent. When someone does not pay on time, evict them immediately! NO EXCUSES!

- Family members can often help a tenant if they can't pay the rent.

1 MINUTE TO RENTAL PROPERTY RICHES

Priorities

When you have low income apartment buildings, there is a continuous turnover of tenants. That means that you are continually looking for new tenants. One of my low income tenants was Laura. Laura looked a lot like my typical tenant. She was a young, single female with 2 kids. She received money from government agencies and this money was not much more than she needed to live. We pick up the story after Laura had lived in our apartment for about 5 months. Up to this point, Laura had always paid her rent on time and I had no reason to believe that this month would be any different.

I began to sense that something was wrong on the afternoon of the 4th. This is the last day to pay rent without a late fee, and I had not been able to contact Laura. I tried to call her several times and received no answer. By about 4pm, I had received the rents from all the other tenants and I was ready to go home. I decided to drive by the apartment to see if Laura was home. Laura was home and she said that her ex-husband had gone to cash her check. He should be back in about 1/2 hour with the rent. I told her that I would be back in 1/2 an hour.

I decided to make a quick trip to MacDonalds to pick up some cookies while I waited. I arrived back at Laura's apartment at 4:45pm and discovered that Laura was gone and Laura's ex-husband was not there. I waited another 15 minutes and finally decided that I had been deceived. I went home.

Early the next morning, I delivered a 3-day notice to vacate the property. Laura was home and I asked her why she had not paid the rent as agreed. She said that she spent $150 on a cell phone and did not have the money. I was not happy! I was especially unhappy that she had lied to me and wasted an entire hour of my time as I was waiting for her ex-husband to bring me the rent the evening before. She knew that he wouldn't be coming back with the rent, but she was just trying to get out of there and avoid telling me the truth.

I had two choices. I could either go through the eviction process or try to get her to leave voluntarily. I asked her if she was willing to leave immediately. She said that I would have to evict her.

In my area, evicting a tenant normally costs us about $800 in court costs and legal fees plus the lost rent. I try to avoid that if there is another alternative.

"Laura", I said, "you have two choices. You can either be out of the apartment with all of your belongings within two days or I am not only going to evict you, but I am IMMEDIATELY GOING TO CALL CHILDREN'S SERVICES. Your children will probably be taken away from you if I am forced to call them. It is YOUR choice. What do you want to do?"

Laura immediately promised to move out within two days!

Two days later, she was out and the place was clean. My tactic worked. I got the tenant out and saved the expensive eviction.

Lessons Learned

- Learn everything you can about your tenants. Many tenants will tell you their life story if you simply ask how they are doing. Learn to be a good listener.

- Be a hands-on landlord. Pick up the rent in person and drive by your properties from time to time. Meet the neighbors if you get the chance and ask them how things are going in the neighborhood. Leave them a business card.

- Be creative in trying to avoid an eviction. In this case, I knew from listening to the tenant that she had been in trouble with Children's Services. When she tried to steal from us by refusing to pay the rent, we were able to successfully get her out by promising to call Children's Services if she didn't leave in 2 days. You notice that I said "promise" to call Children's Services and not "threaten" to call Children's Services, because I absolutely would have done it if she was not out as I instructed.

- Never try to bluff tenants. When you say something, you MUST follow through or you will lose all credibility as a landlord.

Tree Trouble

Although most of the nightmare stories associated with landlording result from bad tenants, that is not always true. One of my many frustrating days started with a large tree that needed to be cut down.

I purchased a small house on a blue collar street. It was in nearly perfect condition, except for a large tree in the front yard. The tree took up a large portion of the front yard. The roots had caused the sidewalk to bulge several inches and had cracked the front porch. Clearly, the tree must come down!

I contacted a local tree company and we agreed on a very reasonable price to remove the tree. The contractor started cutting down the large tree late one afternoon. Just before dark, I stopped by the property to see how they were doing with the tree.

1 MINUTE TO RENTAL PROPERTY RICHES

To my dismay, the owner of the tree company had gone home and only a couple of workers remained. The tree was about half cut down with one of the two forks of the tree still standing. Branches covered almost half of the street and completely blocked the alley and sidewalk. I told the workers that they could not leave the branches blocking the street or alley and they agreed. They said that they would put all of the branches in the front yard, although I did not see how that was possible due to the small size of the yard. I asked if they had any cones or marking tape to place around the sidewalk that surely would be blocked. They did not. At this point, I volunteered to go to Lowes to pick up some caution tape.

By the time I returned from Lowes with the tape, it was dark. The workers had all left. They had removed the branches from the street, but had left a HUGH pile of branches blocking the alley and sidewalk. I could not believe it. I specifically told them not to block the street or the alley. Besides the risk of an accident, the city would surely have something to say about this. I placed the caution tape around the alley and the sidewalk. I then called the owner of the tree company and expressed my dissatisfaction with the way that the property was left. The owner assured me that the mess would be taken care of first thing the next morning.

The next morning, I went to the property at about 10am to check on the status of the work. I was shocked to see that the previous day's mess was still there and that branches once again blocked the street. Only two workers were there and they were getting into their truck as I was arriving. I asked them where they were going. They said that the city inspector had stopped by the property and ordered them to stop work. Apparently, the contractor did not have a license to work in the city and did not have the proper permit to cut down the tree. I insisted that they clean up the hugh piles of branches, but they refused. They said that the city inspector said that they must immediately leave the site or they would be arrested.

Needless to say, this left me in quite a predicament. The workers left the property and I was left with a hugh mess. I spent the rest of the day cleaning up the mess that the workers had caused. I had to rent a chipper to get rid of the branches and had to take care of the logs that they left. I was worried all day that the police or city inspector would stop by and cite me for something, but fortunately nothing happened. The neighbors were not happy about the mess, but they understood that a good contractor is hard to find. Needless to say, I didn't pay the "contractor" and did not use him anymore.

Lessons Learned

- Ensure that all contractors are properly licensed.

- Know you state and local laws. In this case, I was unaware that our city prohibited cutting down trees on private property without a permit.

1 MINUTE TO RENTAL PROPERTY RICHES

Two for the Money

In my business, we tend to do multiple deals at once. On this occasion, we were taking over two 4-unit apartment buildings. Seven of the eight total units were already occupied. All the paperwork had been done; the deeds were transferred; and the money had changed hands. I was excited.

In an effort to make a smooth transition from the previous owner to our company, I arranged to have the previous owner take me around to pick up the rents and be introduced to the tenants. The first tenant was not home and the previous landlord had already received his rent, which she would be giving to me. The second tenant was a woman named Jean. I was introduced to Jean and picked up the rent. Next door to Jean was Jamal. We knocked on the door and Jamal opened the door. I was introduced by the previous landlord and asked for the rent. "I don't have it", said Jamal. "I have applied for worker's comp and should have a check in two or three weeks". I explained to Jamal that we did not accept excuses for not paying the rent. He either had to pay or be evicted. He refused to pay. The final apartment in this building was vacant.

We moved down the street to the next building. The first tenant was a lady on Section 8. I had already received her check from Section 8, but we stopped there so that I could meet her. The next apartment was a middle aged man named Doug. Doug came to the door and announced that he was moving immediately. He had already started moving his belongings and would be out by the end of the day. I was a little dismayed that 2 of the 7 tenants were not paying rent. I had not expected that and we still had two apartments to go.

The final two apartments were upstairs. These apartments shared a common electric meter and the landlord had rented both units to one tenant. This tenant was subletting one of the apartments to another man. This unit was a mess. The people lived like pigs and there were about 5 dogs in the apartment. We knocked on the door of the primary renter. His wife answered the door. She said that her husband had beaten her up and that he was in jail. She was moving and would not pay the rent. I explained to her that she had to pay the rent and give a 30-day notice to move. "Evict me", she said. She was not paying for either upstairs apartment.

In the period of only 30 minutes, I went from the proud new owner of two apartment buildings that were almost fully rented, to a very agitated owner of two buildings that were largely filled with non-paying tenants. I was NOT HAPPY! I had an uneasy feeling in the pit of my stomach. In fact, I felt downright SICK!

I went home to lick my wounds and to prepare all the 3-day eviction notices for the next day. At this point in my career, I had dozens of rental units and was by no means a new landlord. I had experienced many tenant nightmares, but they usually occurred one at a time.

1 MINUTE TO RENTAL PROPERTY RICHES

I had known the seller of the buildings since grade school. She is a very honest person and a good Christian. However, her kind heart was now the source of my problem. After talking with her, I discovered that she became a landlord with the intent of helping people. While that is a noble goal, it is not compatible with running a successful real estate rental business. Both of these buildings were full of down-and-outers. In fact, I was later to find out that all but two of the tenants were drug addicts, and two were drug dealers!

The next morning, I delivered 3-day eviction notices to the four non-paying tenants. After delivering the eviction notices, I began working on one of the buildings. The exterior of the building was filthy and I wanted to wash it down and then paint it. As I began working, I noticed a steady stream of people going into apartments #2 and #3. Cars would pull up, a nasty looking person would go into apartment #2 and then apartment #3. Each person would only stay about 3 minutes and then would leave. In the first hour that I worked on the building, there must have been twenty people come and go. It was clear that this was a crack house! To make matters worse, the tenants involved were two of the three tenants that had paid their rent. They would clearly have to go, so that meant that only one tenant out of the original seven would be staying. Now I was really depressed!

I knocked on the door of apartment #2. I asked the tenant, Jean, to come outside for a moment. "I know what is going on here and we are NOT going to have a crack house operating on the property!" "They are only visiting" was her reply. "There is nothing illegal about having friends….is there?"

With that, I knew exactly where we stood. Jean had every intention of running a crack house and she was playing me for stupid.

Just after talking with Jean, the next door neighbor came over to speak to me. Harvey introduced himself. He had owned the house next door for nearly fifty years. I asked him if he had observed any trouble with the tenants of the building. "It has been a crack house for five years. The drug addicts have been terrorizing us for all that time and we can't seem to get anything done. We've called the police again and again and nothing ever happens. Things are a mess."

I told Harvey that things were about to change. I promised to clean up the building and get rid of all the druggies. I would clean, repair, and paint the building. I would find some good tenants.

Harvey seemed pleased that there was at least some hope that things would change. I gave Harvey my business card and invited him to call me if there were any problems at the building.

1 MINUTE TO RENTAL PROPERTY RICHES

I decided that I should figure out who I had inherited as tenants. I did a computer check of Jean and found out that she had a lengthy criminal history, including a felony conviction for drug trafficking. The other tenant was a known drug addict and had spent time in a mental institution. I HAD GOTTEN MYSELF INTO A MESS!

The next day, I started my new mission with a trip to the police station. I talked to the police Captain and told him what was going on at the apartment building. I asked if they could increase the patrols and I expressed my desire that they perform a drug bust. After talking to the police, I called our local drug task force and explained the situation to them. Again, I asked them to perform a drug bust and throw my problem tenants in jail.

A few days after taking over the building, I received a call by one of the neighbors at about 9pm. "I think that you should get down here right away. There are four police cars in front of your building." I rushed down to the property to find police all over the place. They had attempted a drug bust. When they entered the apartment, they found a crack pipe and some crack. However, they did not arrest anyone because the druggies had set the crack pipe and crack on the table just before they entered the property and they could not prove whose crack and crack pipe it was. Needless to say, I was quite frustrated!

A couple of days later, there was a big fight at the building. Once again the neighbors called me, this time at midnight. I rushed down to the property to discover that the police had arrested some of the drug addicts that were hanging around in Jean's apartment after they got into a fight. Unfortunately, Jean was not among those that were arrested.

The very next day, the police were once again at the apartment. This time they were there to see Jimmy, who was the crack addict in apartment #3. Jimmy had called the police because he gave a drug dealer money for crack and the drug dealer didn't give Jimmy the drugs. I absolutely could not believe it. Are these drug addicts so stupid that they would call the police to complain that a drug dealer cheated them out of some crack? YES, THEY ARE! I went to the police station and received a copy of the police report. It was right there in black and white. Jimmy filed a complaint with the police that he had been cheated out of crack!

A day later, Jean's husband got out of prison and returned to our building. I didn't even know that Jean was married. Her husband had a long criminal history with four felonies and exactly fifty (yes 50) misdemeanors. Many of these crimes were for violent acts.

A couple of days later, the police were once again at the building. Jean's husband had beaten her up and she called the police. She literally threw his clothes into the alley and kicked him out.

1 MINUTE TO RENTAL PROPERTY RICHES

Over the next few weeks, there were dozens of incidents at the building. Crack was being sold nearly every minute of every day. Every single night was a big crack party. You could clearly see the crack pipes being lit even through the curtains. Every loser within fifty miles must have visited my crack house. I received frequent calls from the neighbors. The neighbors and I called the police and the drug task force nearly every day.

By the end of the first month, I had nearly 50 pages of police reports. Unfortunately, neither Jean or Jimmy were convicted of a crime. It would be difficult to evict them without absolute proof that a crime had been committed. However, something HAD to be done. I had been through a WILD month, the neighbors were upset, and I could not expect to fill the building with quality tenants when there was a full blown crack house in operation.

I decided to write up a 30-day eviction notice based on an entire array of factors. I included drug abuse, drug trafficking, fighting, associating with known criminals, and conducting illegal activities at the property. On the 4th, I knocked on Jean's door. When she answered, I told her that she was being evicted. I purposely gave her a hard time. "I'm sick and tired of all the drama", I told her. "You are a drug addict, a troublemaker, and I'm tired of all the scum continuously hanging around your apartment. I have called the drug task force and will personally see to it that you are arrested and sent back to prison!"

She was furious! She cursed at me and was clearly very agitated.

"One more thing", I said. "You owe the rent for this month and I'm here to collect."

"I'm not paying! You can just evict me," was her reply.

With that, I knew I had won. By refusing to pay the rent, she had given me a sure way to evict her. It is often difficult to evict for drug abuse, fighting, or illegal activity. This is especially true if there has not been a conviction. However, evicting someone for non-payment of rent is VERY EASY. She would be out in about a month. At least there was light at the end of the tunnel.

As planned, after another month of misery, we finally had the court date and Jean was evicted. A few days later, she moved out and was gone. Believe it or not, Jean was accepted into a government assisted housing complex, where she continued dealing drugs. The drug task force finally caught up with her and she was arrested. She is currently awaiting trial on felony drug charges.

1 MINUTE TO RENTAL PROPERTY RICHES

Lessons Learned

Unfortunately, I learned some hard lessons with the purchase of these two buildings. You should learn from my mistakes so that you won't have to learn these lessons the hard way.

- It is absolutely critical that you screen tenants in buildings that you buy, just as if they are new tenant applicants. Especially important is the criminal background check for inherited tenants. You want to know who you'll be getting.

- Another trick is to get a copy of the police reports for your new building. By doing so, you might uncover criminal activity that is ongoing at the property, but that has not yet resulted in the arrest of your tenant.

- It is also a good idea to talk to the neighbors around any property that you are considering buying. You may not only uncover problems with the existing tenants, but you may get critical information about the neighborhood and street.

- <u>Always review the leases for any tenants that are in a building that you are about to buy. Remember that tenants have rights as spelled out in their lease and a new owner does not change their lease. It is especially important to determine the length of leases that are in place. It is possible that a tenant could have a 30-year lease at a ridiculously low rent. You would be obligated by this lease! Check all leases</u>!

Conclusion

These landlord horror stories are typical. In fact, I've only included a small number of the incidents that I've personally experienced. These nightmare stories are the rule for all serious landlords, not the exception. You should be prepared to deal with these types of situations and still be able to sleep at night.

Keep in mind that the vast majority of tenants are good people. Approximately 90% of my tenants cause no trouble at all. At any given time, about 10% of the tenants are some trouble, but usually nothing too serious. In my business, we evict about 1% of our tenants each month. These are the tenants from which these horror stories come.

SPEAKING TENANTESE

Every profession has its own unique language. In real estate, there are a variety of terms that a savvy investor will know. Terms like Cash Flow, Operating Expenses, Net Operating Income, Depreciation, Appreciation, and Sub 2, are just a few of the terms that are common in this business.

Landlords also have a specific language that they must learn if they are to be successful. It is certainly beyond the scope of this book to teach you the complete language, but I will attempt to give you some of the key phrases of this language. The language that I am speaking of is Tenantese, the language of your tenants. Believe me, what tenants say and what they mean can be two completely different things. Below are some key phrases in Tenantese followed by their translation in English.

- Tenantese: Could I plant some flowers?

  English: I am a complete slob and am planning to completely trash your property.

- Tenantese: My grandmother died and I spent the rent money going to the funeral.

  English: I spent the rent on a big screen TV.

- Tenantese: The transmission went out on my truck and I had to get it fixed.

  English: I spent the rent on a $400 dog.

- Tenantese: My only criminal record was from when I was a kid.

  English: I got arrested for assault last year (when I was a 26 year old kid).

- Tenantese: I haven't been in trouble for over 6 years.

  English: I just got out of prison after serving 6 years for armed robbery.

1 MINUTE TO RENTAL PROPERTY RICHES

- Tenantese: Do you mind if I baby sit my sister's kids once in a while?

  English: I am planning to operate an illegal day care center in your rental.

- Tenantese: Can I get a puppy?

  English: I just bought a Pit Bull!

- Tenantese: Will you work with me on the security deposit?

  English: I don't work, I have no money, and I certainly will never pay the security deposit.

- Tenantese: I'll be starting a new job next week.

  English: I just got fired from my last job, where I worked almost a week.

- Tenantese: I am looking for an apartment that is available right away.

  English: I just got evicted!

- Tenantese: What are the requirements to rent your house?

  English: I have something to hide and want to know if you'll find it.

- Tenantese: My friend is just visiting.

  English: My friend just moved in.

- Tenantese: I'm sorry. There won't be any more problems.

  English: There won't be any more trouble while you're standing here.

The point in presenting these tenant translations is to illustrate the wide variety of lies you will be told by your tenants and tenant applicants. If you are a normal middle or upper class person, chances are good that you have not been exposed to these kinds of people in the past. I can guarantee that you will be shocked at the frequency and extent of lies that you will be hearing. There is an entire segment of our population that lives very differently than you and I do.

So, the moral of the story here is to verify everything that you are told. Never accept ANYTHING at face value. My father was in supervision for many years at a major US manufacturer. One of the things that he has told me frequently is that "people do what you inspect, not what you expect." These are very wise words from someone with a lot of experience managing people. This bit of wisdom could be converted to our landlording business as follows: "believe what you verify, not what you hear." Verify everything that you hear from tenants and tenant applicants, starting your very first day in business. Many new landlords learn this the hard way.

APARTMENT BUILDINGS AND COMPLEXES

This is actually a bonus chapter that was not included in the original e-book. I did not include this chapter in the original e-book because I don't recommend that new landlords start with apartments. For the reasons already outlined in this book, it is strongly advised that all new landlords begin their investing career with single family houses.

Why Invest In Apartment Buildings and Complexes?

I own many apartment buildings. They can be great investments and there are many positive aspects to owning multi-unit buildings.

One of the best reasons to buy apartment buildings is that you can more quickly build your rental property business. To acquire 50 rentals, you could either buy fifty single family houses or five 10-unit buildings or one 50-unit apartment complex. Obviously, it takes a lot more work to find; arrange financing for; buy; and manage fifty individual houses than to do a single deal for one apartment complex. To many new investors, buying an apartment building seems like hitting the lottery. It offers the lure of a get rich quick scheme because everything can presumably be done instantly. In reality, there is some truth to that idea. IF (and that's a BIG IF), a new investor can find an apartment building or complex at a large discount; get financing for the deal; and then successfully manage the building or complex, then it is certainly possible to make a lot of money.

Another great factor with apartment buildings is that your investments are located in fewer locations. Instead of having houses spread all over town, your rentals can be located in only a few (or even one) location. This makes it easier to manage your business.

Apartment buildings and complexes can be more efficient than houses. Instead of having fifty roofs, you may only have one roof. Instead of fifty yards, you may only have one yard. Instead of fifty driveways, you may only have one. This can make your business much more efficient and this will save you money.

Most of us only have so much money. That's why we got into the rental property business to start with - TO MAKE MONEY! Additionally, most of us only have the ability to borrow a finite amount of money in a given period of time. At some point, the bank becomes nervous and won't want to loan any more money, at least in the near term. Apartment buildings offer an advantage here also, because they offer a lower price per rental unit. In my area, a typical rental house purchased at a big discount would cost $25,000 to $40,000. A typical rental unit in an apartment building in my area, also purchased at a big discount, runs about $14,000 per unit! Stated another way, you get more bang for your buck with apartment buildings.

1 MINUTE TO RENTAL PROPERTY RICHES

When my laundry is dirty, I take it to the laundry room in my house. Most apartment dwellers do not have a washer and dryer. They go to the nearest laundry mat. This provides an excellent opportunity for owners of apartment buildings to make some extra money. If the apartment building has the space, coin-operated laundry machines can be installed. Additionally, you might also consider putting in some vending machines.

Special Considerations with Apartment Buildings and Complexes

Apartment buildings sound GREAT - don't they? Unfortunately, to this point we've only discussed the rosy side of apartment buildings. Like many people, apartment buildings have two sides - a good side and a bad side.

Let's start with the tenants. There is a specific pecking order in life. On one extreme, the rich live in their multi-million dollar mansions. On the other extreme, people are homeless and literally live in the street. Only one step above the homeless are low-income apartment dwellers. Many of these people constantly live on the fringe of society. They don't work. They are on welfare and public assistance. They have criminal histories. They are often mentally ill. They have drug and alcohol addictions. They live soap opera lives.

When you choose to manage apartment buildings, especially low income apartment buildings, you enter this world of shady characters and will be dealing with these troubled people. Low income apartment dwellers are the most difficult tenants to deal with and most people simply can not deal with the stress! In fact, the stress of dealing with terrible tenants is the number two reason that new rental property businesses fail, second only to a lack of cash flow.

Due to many factors, including the size and expense or these projects, and the poor quality of tenants associated with apartment buildings, owners of apartment buildings tend to be more sophisticated. They tend to be professional investors as opposed to the mom-and-pop type investors often associated with single family houses. This creates many problems for the new landlord that is trying to get into the apartment building business. For one thing, these sophisticated buyers know the value of property. They are not likely to sell you their building at a big discount. When they do sell, they look for a newbie to sell to at retail.

There are far fewer apartment buildings than single family houses and the demand for apartment buildings is much less than for houses. Therefore, if the new owner of an apartment building wants or needs to sell, there is a MUCH smaller market for the building. Combine the small market with the fact that the buyers are more sophisticated (and therefore want to buy at a big discount), and you can see that apartment buildings can be difficult to sell. In fact, they can be VERY DIFFICULT TO SELL.

Apartment buildings have expenses that do not exist with single family rentals. For example, apartment buildings often have lobbies, hallways, swimming pools, laundry rooms, etc. These areas are called common areas because all of the tenants may use them. Since they are not leased to a single tenant, these areas will need to be cleaned and taken care of by the landlord. Common areas may also have lights and heat that are on a separate electric meter, which is also paid by the landlord. Finally, the lawn mowing and snow removal is also the responsibility of the landlord with apartment buildings.

Money Talks

Things can be a lot more expensive with apartment buildings than houses. For example, an appraisal on a house might typically cost $350. You won't find an appraisal on an apartment building or apartment complex for $350! On a small apartment building, an appraisal might cost $1,500. An appraisal for an apartment complex could easily cost many thousands of dollars. Maintenance and upgrades can also be much more expensive. Larger apartment buildings (over 3 units in Ohio) are considered commercial property. These commercial buildings have different building laws than residential property. For example, here in Ohio, an owner can do electrical work on his own 3 unit building. A licensed commercial electrician is required to work on any building with more than 3 units. Likewise, plans are required to be drawn and approved for certain commercial projects which are not required for 1-3 unit buildings. These different requirements can have a drastic impact on the budget for maintenance and upgrade work that needs to be done. You should do some research to determine the cost impact of owning commercial property in your area!

Many states also have different rules for apartment buildings once they reach a certain size. For example, some states require an on-site manager for buildings with more than 10 units.

Finally, there is a significant difference in the loans that are used for commercial and residential rental property. Typically, rental houses are financed with familiar 30 year mortgages, just like your home mortgage. Commercial properties usually are financed with a different class of loan products. A typical commercial loan might have a 20 year term, with a 5 year ARM, and a balloon payment in 10 years.

All of these issues deserve some attention from the investor who is serious about investing in apartment buildings. It is essential that you be fully educated on the details of any investment that you contemplate.

1 MINUTE TO RENTAL PROPERTY RICHES

Special Terminology

I mentioned earlier that investors in apartment buildings and apartment complexes were usually a little more sophisticated than the average investor in single family houses. These professional investors also use some additional terminology that most SFH investors don't use.

Cap Rate (Capitalization Rate)

You will frequently hear investors talk about the cap rate of a property. Cap rate is defined as the Net Operating Income (NOI) divided by the value of the property. Therefore if you know the average Cap Rate for the area, also called the Market Capitalization Rate, you can theoretically determine the value of a property if you know the NOI. You will remember from earlier in this book that NOI is defined as Gross Rents minus Operating Expenses. Therefore, to determine the value of a property using Cap Rate, you simply divide the NOI by the Cap Rate.

So, what does all this Cap Rate talk really tell us - NOT MUCH! Basically, it <u>attempts</u> to tell us what a particular property is worth based on what other investors paid for their property. Unfortunately, most investors overpay for their property. The vast majority of new rental property businesses fail. So, one could argue that the cap rate really only tells us how much the failures paid for their property. Additionally, because cap rate is based on the NOI, the question is who provided the expense information and the corresponding NOI? The sellers? A realtor? An appraiser? The vast majority of sellers underestimate the expenses with rental properties. The vast majority of realtors know absolutely nothing about the expenses associated with rental properties. So, what confidence should you place in Cap Rate? NONE!

Gross Rent Multiplier (GRM)

Gross Rent Multiplier is another attempt to determine the value of a property based on other sales in the area. To determine the gross rent multiplier for the area, the sales prices are compared to the gross rents of the properties. The gross rent multiplier is simply sales price divided by gross rent.

For example a rental property recently sold for $100,000 and had gross monthly rents of $1,000 per month. The gross rent multiplier would by $100,000 divided by $1,000 = 100. This property would have a gross rent multiplier of 100. The theory is that if you know the gross rent multiplier for the area, you can determine the value of a rental property by simply knowing the gross rents. Let's say that you find a rental property with gross rents of $5,000 per month and you know that the gross rent multiplier for the area is 100. Using this theory, the property would be worth $500,000 ($5,000 multiplied by 100).

1 MINUTE TO RENTAL PROPERTY RICHES

I have the same objections to GRM that I had with Cap Rate. Who determines the gross rent multiplier for the area? What does this really tell you? Again, the answer is NOTHING! If anything, it tells you what the failures paid for their properties.

Cost Per Unit or Cost Per Square Foot

Many investors in apartment buildings will talk about the Cost Per Unit or Cost Per Square Foot. Cost Per Unit is simply the price of an apartment building divided by the number of apartments. Cost Per Square Foot is simply the price of an apartment building divided by the number of square feet in the building. What does this tell you about the profitability of the building? NOTHING! What does this tell you about the amount you should pay for a property? NOTHING!

Debt Service Coverage Ratio (DSCR), also known as Debt Coverage Ratio

Debt Service Coverage Ratio is another term used by so-called sophisticated investors. It is determined by dividing the NOI by the Debt (mortgage) for the property. If the DSCR is greater than 1, it means that the property will have a positive cash flow. If the DSCR is less than 1, the cash flow is negative. This is useful information, but in my opinion this is still a silly term used by people who want to appear to be sophisticated. What we really want to know is not whether a property has a positive cash flow, but rather HOW MUCH the positive cash flow will be. So, instead of calculating DSCR, why not simply subtract the mortgage payment from the NOI? The result is our actual cash flow, which is infinitely more useful than determining the DSCR.

I could go on and on with these silly terms. Some other examples are Discounted Cash Flows, Internal Rate of Return, Modified Internal Rate of Return, and Net Income Multiplier. I'm not going to waste any more space defining them. If you're interested, simply Google them.

I have successfully owned and operated businesses for over 15 years. One thing I can tell you from experience is that the formula for being successful in any business is just not that complicated. Get out your highlighter! Here is the "SECRET" to being successful in any business: YOU MUST TAKE IN MORE MONEY THAN GOES OUT! Said another way, you must have positive cash flow! It's not much of a secret, but that is the truth. Knowing a bunch of fancy terms won't do one thing to improve your cash flow, but it does sound good at parties.

1 MINUTE TO RENTAL PROPERTY RICHES

Realistic Purchase Considerations

There are really two primary considerations in purchasing any property, whether it's a single family house or a 100 unit apartment complex.

The first consideration is CASH FLOW. By this point in the book, I hope that you understand that having a Positive Cash Flow is the most important requirement for any property that you purchase. If you don't have positive cash flow, you are on the fast track to going out of business!

The second consideration is Equity. You should buy every property at a discount so that you have equity in the property. Equity is wealth. Equity is also your insurance that you can sell at a discount if you need or want to get out of the property.

Purchase Criteria

You should use the very same criteria for purchasing apartment buildings and apartment complexes that you use for single family houses. These were covered in detail earlier in this book. Those criteria are:

1. Buy all properties at a maximum of 70% of the market value.
2. Buy all properties with a minimum positive cash flow of at least $100 per unit per month.
3. Buy all properties so that the monthly gross rents are at least 2% of your cost of the property (purchase price + rehab costs).

I hope that you now realize that buying apartment buildings and apartment complexes is the same as buying smaller rental properties. While there are a few unique aspects to apartment buildings, all of the same basic considerations apply. If you buy so that you will have positive cash flow and equity, you will be successful regardless of what you buy.

NOW WHAT?

You now have a big decision to make. You have completed this book, which is a thorough look at the real world of landlording. You have all of the information that you need to get started. It is at exactly this point that the vast majority of potential investors give up. There are a variety of reasons for this phenomenon. Some people lack motivation. Others over-analyze things and simply can not make a decision. Yet others are paralyzed with fear of failing.

I have heard the real estate gurus say that 95% of people buying their courses never do anything with them. Many of these courses simply sit on the shelf. Keep in mind that these are students who have been highly motivated at a seminar and have spent hundreds or thousands on the guru's course.

Deciding not to pursue a rental property business may not be a bad decision. You have been given all of the facts in this book and I have not attempted to sugar coat them. Starting any business is a lot of work and carries a high probability of failure. Owners of new business usually work far more hours than those with a job. Additionally, new business owners often must go for years without a vacation as their new business gets up and running.

So, why would anyone in their right mind decide to start a rental property business? The answer is simple, there is absolutely nothing that compares to being your own boss. When you own a business, you can decide when to work and what to do. There is no boss to ask for a day off and no one to set deadlines for you. If you have a cold or the flu, you can stay home. If a family member needs help, you can be there. If you wake up and decide to do nothing today, you can do that. If you want to start work at 5am, you can to that too. You are completely in charge and that is something that you can never get as an employee! IT IS WONDERFUL! Once you've experienced the freedom of being the owner, it is nearly impossible to go back to the rat race of a 9 to 5 job.

Another big advantage to starting a business, is that your income is no longer limited. With most jobs, you make a relatively fixed amount of money. Sure, you could work some overtime and make a little extra. However, the maximum that you can make is determined by the number of hours you can work. With a rental property business, your income is unlimited. If you want to make $10,000 per month, you might need to own 50 to 100 rental units. If you want to make $20,000 per month, you might need to own 100 to 200 rental units. Your income is not limited in any way.

1 MINUTE TO RENTAL PROPERTY RICHES

At the same time you're building your income with rentals, you will also be building your wealth. I can think of no other business where it is entirely possible to go from zero net worth to being a millionaire in five years or less. Simply buying the properties at a discount and allowing the tenants to pay down your mortgage will cause your net worth to rapidly increase. The vast majority of employees will never be a millionaire.

So, what are you going to do NOW? If your decision is to start a rental property business, then you need to get started. Set some goals and write them down. I have included a goal sheet in the appendix for this purpose. Goals are worthless without including a time frame. You should set a date that each goal will be met. I would suggest completing the goal sheet TODAY.

After setting your goals, start working your way through the ACTION CHECKLIST. This is a list of some critical tasks that must be completed as you begin your new business. The items on this list do not need to be accomplished in the order they are listed. However, they do need to be completed.

You are about to embark on a wonderful journey - the journey to FREEDOM. Freedom from the 9 to 5 rat race; freedom to earn to your potential; and freedom to lead your own life!

I wish you the best of luck.

Happy Investing!

OTHER PRODUCTS

Coaching/Mentoring

I am generally not in favor of hiring a coach or mentor. In my opinion, these are services that the new investor should be able to get for free at their local REIA. In most cases, the best coach or mentor is simply a local, successful investor with whom you can become friends. These experienced investors are often willing to assist new investors for free. They know the local market and local issues.

If you have difficulty learning from books and need a little extra help, I do offer limited coaching/mentoring. As I said at the beginning of the book, I am a full time real estate investor and landlord, not a professional speaker or mentor. I make my living actually being a landlord.

However, if you need a little help and want to be coached/mentored by me, please send me an e-mail at mike@1minutetorentalpropertyriches.com. If you decide to pursue coaching/mentoring, all of your interactions will be with me personally, either by e-mail or telephone. Also, I only do coaching/mentoring on a monthly basis. Either you or I can cancel our agreement at any time. If your are interested in coaching/mentoring, send me an e-mail.

ADDITIONS AND CORRECTIONS

We have made every effort to ensure that this book is complete and error free. It is our intention that this book become THE comprehensive text on landlording. We hope that you have found it to be an excellent resource and that the information it contains will literally change your life.

If you find any errors or would like to see additional topics covered, please send the author an e-mail at mike@1minutetorentalpropertyriches.com. As we revise the book, we will make every attempt to address your suggestions.

We also welcome critiques! If you have any feedback for us, good or bad, please feel free to e-mail at the same address.

Thank You!

APPENDIX

This appendix contains all of the forms, leases, and contracts that I routinely use in the operation of my rental property business. Most of these forms can be used exactly as they are presented. Simply copy them and they are ready to use!

Other forms may need to be modified to be legal and effective in your particular state. Every state has it's own Tenant-Landlord Laws and your leases and contracts must reflect the current law. I have not attempted to include forms for every state because all forms are potentially obsolete the minute they are printed. The main reason that documents can become obsolete is that laws are continually changing. Therefore, **IT IS ABSOLUTELY NECESSARY THAT YOU VERIFY THE LEGALITY AND SUITABILITY OF ALL FORMS, LEASES, AND CONTRACTS IN THIS BOOK FOR USE IN YOUR STATE.** I suggest checking with an experienced real estate attorney, your local REIA, or an experienced investor in your area to verify that these leases and forms will work in your area.

1 MINUTE TO RENTAL PROPERTY RICHES

Goals Worksheet

Long Term Goal

1. Income: my goal is to build my business until I have a monthly income of $_____. I will reach this goal by _____. (date)

2. Equity: my goal is to build my business until I have equity in my rental properties of $_____. I will reach this goal by _____. (date)

Short Term Goals:

1. To reach my long term goals, I will buy _____ rental units per year starting in _____. (month/year)

2. Before I can buy my first house, I need to complete my basic real estate education. This will include reading books on specific purchasing techniques that interest me, such as sub 2, owner financing, lease-option, etc. My basic education also includes studying my state's Tenant-Landlord Law; joining my local REIA; and verifying that my contracts, forms, and leases are appropriate to my state. I will complete my basic education by _____ (date).

3. I also need to become an expert in my local market. To do this, I will look at a minimum of 100 houses that are for sale. I will complete this task by _____ (date).

4. Part of becoming a successful investor is to assemble a team of professionals to work with me. This team will consist of a realtor, banker, title agency, real estate lawyer, and accountant or other tax professional. I will identify the members of my team by _____ (date).

5. I plan to buy my first rental property by _____ (date).

ACTION CHECKLIST

Date
Completed

_____   Identify your target investment area

_____   Look at 100 houses that are on the market (inside and out) in your target area

_____   Obtain a copy of your state's Tenant-Landlord Laws

_____   Join your local Real Estate Investors Association (REIA)

_____   Find a realtor to locate properties for you

_____   Find a lawyer that specializes in real estate and evictions

_____   Find a title company that works with investors

_____   Subscribe to the local newspaper and start looking at the ads

_____   Check with a lawyer or a successful investor in your area to determine if all of your forms are appropriate for your state.

_____   Arrange for financing from a small local bank

_____   Make offers on appropriate property using the formulas in this book

_____   Arrange for Insurance Coverage

_____   Purchase your first rental property

_____   Place a "For Rent" ad in your local newspaper

_____   Place a "For Rent" ad in the yard or window of your rental property

_____   Thoroughly screen potential tenants

_____   Follow the Leasing Checklist to sign up your first tenant

Congratulations, you are now a landlord!

1 MINUTE TO RENTAL PROPERTY RICHES

CASH FLOW SHEET

Gross Rents _____

Subtract Operating Expenses _____
(1/2 of Gross Rents)

= Net Operating Income _____

Subtract Mortgage Payment _____
(Principal and Interest)

= Cash flow _____

To determine cash flow for a property, subtract the operating expenses (1/2 of the gross rents) from the gross rents. This gives you Net Operating Income. Then subtract the Mortgage Payment (principal and interest) and the result is the cash flow. If the cash flow is positive, you should expect to make money. If the result is negative, then the property will lose money.

CALCULATING MAXIMUM PURCHASE PRICE

1. Calculate maximum purchase price per the following 70% rule:

Market Value   _____

Multiply by .7   x .70

=   _____

Subtract Repairs   _____

= Maximum Purchase Price   _____ (by 70% rule)

2. Calculate maximum purchase price per the 2% rule

Gross Rent   _____

Divide by .02   /.02

=   _____

Subtract Repairs   _____

= Maximum Purchase Price   _____ (by 2% rule)

THE MOST YOU SHOULD PAY FOR A PROPERTY IS THE <u>LOWER</u> VALUE OF MAXIMUM PURCHASE PRICE AS DETERMINED BY STEPS 1 AND 2 ABOVE.

PROPERTY PURCHASE CHECKLIST

_____ Purchase contract signed by both buyer and seller

_____ Obtain financing

_____ Perform any inspections per the contract (termite, gas line, mold, etc)

_____ Title Search

_____ Order Title Insurance

_____ Survey (if desired)

_____ Review Settlement (HUD) Statement the day before the closing

_____ Get a certified check for any funds that you need to take to the closing

_____ Do a final walk-through of the property before closing (to be sure no damage has occurred)

_____ Go to Closing

_____ Get the keys, garage door openers, etc from the seller

_____ Record the Deed (or be sure the deed is recorded)

_____ Be certain that you receive your title insurance policy

REAL ESTATE PURCHASE CONTRACT

ONCE SIGNED BY BOTH PARTIES, THIS DOCUMENT BECOMES A LEGALLY BINDING CONTRACT. IF THE TERMS OF THIS CONTRACT ARE NOT FULLY UNDERSTOOD, THEN LEGAL OR OTHER ADVICE SHOULD BE SOUGHT FROM A COMPETENT PROFESSIONAL BEFORE SIGNING.

The Seller(s), _____ of _____(address) hereby agrees to sell to the Buyer, _____ of _____(address), the real property described below and all improvements thereon (herein referred to as the Property), and Buyer agrees to purchase said Property from the Seller on the terms and conditions set forth in this contract.

DESCRIPTION: The Property is located in _____County, _____ (city/state) and is commonly known as_____
_____
_____

PURCHASE PRICE: The Buyer agrees to pay for and the Seller agrees to sell said property on the following terms Purchase price shall be $_____.
Buyer's obligations are contingent upon :_____
_____
_____
_____
_____

_____(buyer/seller) will pay for survey, appraisal fee, title search, real estate commission of buyer's agent, F.H.A./V.A. mortgage discount, Lead paint inspection, home inspection, repairs or replacements required by the F.H.A. or V.A. , termite inspection, and recordation of deed.

PRORATED ITEMS: All rents, taxes, assessments, and prepaid insurance premiums shall be prorated as of the date of closing.

TITLE: Seller at _____ cost shall deliver to Buyer a good and sufficient Warranty Deed with appropriate release of dower conveying good and marketable title to the subject premises to the Buyer free and clear of all liens and encumbrances except taxes set forth above (prorated items), restrictions and conditions of record, utility easements, and right of way grants of record, and applicable building or zoning restrictions or regulations. If title evidence or survey reveal any title defect or condition which is not acceptable to the Buyer, the buyer shall notify the Seller within fourteen (14) days of such title defects and Seller agrees to use reasonable efforts to remedy such defects and shall have thirty (30) days to do so, in which case this sale shall be closed within ten (10) days after delivery of acceptable evidence to Buyer that such defects have been cured. Seller agrees to pay for and clear all delinquent taxes, liens, and other encumbrances: otherwise the Buyer shall have the right to cancel this contract and the Seller shall return all deposit(s) to the Buyer, whereupon all rights and liabilities of the parties to this contract shall cease.

POSSESSION: Possession of said property shall be given to Buyer on or before _____, 20_____. Seller shall pay, through date of possession, all accrued utility charges and other charges that are or may become a lien.

CLOSING: Closing of this transaction shall be at the office of _____ on or before _____, 20_____.

DEFAULT BY BUYER: If the Buyer fails to perform the agreements of this contract within the time set forth herein, the Seller may retain as the Seller's exclusive and sole remedy, as liquidated damages and not as a penalty, all of the initial deposit specified above.

DEFAULT BY SELLER: If the Seller fails to perform any of the agreements of this contract, all deposits made above shall be returned to the Buyer and the Buyer shall retain the right to pursue all other legal remedies including legal action seeking specific performance of the contract by the Seller.

Initials: Buyer(s)_____ _____ Seller(s)_____ _____

CONDITION OF THE PROPERTY: The Seller agrees to deliver the Property to the Buyer at closing in its condition at the time of viewing by the buyer.

PERSONAL PROPERTY INCLUDED IN THE PURCHASE PRICE: The following personal property is being sold by the Seller to the Buyer, and shall be delivered to the Buyer at closing._____
_____
_____
_____
_____.

DURATION OF OFFER: This offer shall terminate if not accepted by both parties on or before _____(mo./day), _____(yr.).

ADDITIONAL TERMS AND CONDITIONS:
    (A) There are no additional agreements, promises, or understandings between the parties except as specifically defined forth in this contract. All changes to this contract must be in writing and signed by both parties.
    (B) The provisions of this contract shall survive the closing and shall not merge in any deed of conveyance herein.
    (C) This agreement shall be construed to be under the laws of the State of _____.

NOTICES: Any notices required to be given by this contract shall be sent to the parties at their addresses listed below, either by personal delivery or by certified mail - return receipt requested. Such notice shall be effective upon delivery or mailing

TIME IS OF THE ESSENCE OF THIS AGREEMENT.

In acceptance whereof, the parties signed their names on the dates set forth below.

Buyer(s): _____   Date: _____

_____

Seller(s): _____   Seller's Date of Acceptance_____

_____

TENANT SCREENING POLICY

1. Tenant applicants and all adults that will be living in the rental must show a picture ID.

2. Tenant applicants must have an income of at least 3 times the rent. Food stamps, welfare, other government assistance, and housing vouchers will count toward this requirement.

3. Tenant applicants must have at least a 6 month job history (for those tenants that are paying rent with their money).

4. Tenant applicants must have given their previous landlord proper notice (normally 30 days).

5. We will NOT accept tenants:

    - that have had an eviction in the past 5 years
    - that have had their utilities shut off within the past year
    - that have had a felony in the past 5 years
    - that have had more than 2 misdemeanors in the past 5 years
    - that have any record of drug activity in the past 5 years

Real Estate Leasing Checklist

[ ] Rental Application
    [ ] Credit Check
    [ ] Criminal Background Check
    [ ] Employment Check
    [ ] Previous Landlord Check
    [ ] Reference Check
[ ] Lease
[ ] Cosigner form
[ ] Pet Addendum
[ ] Property Modification Agreement
[ ] Paint Addendum
[ ] Move-In/Move-Out Form
[ ] Emergency Contact Form
[ ] Lead Paint Disclosure
[ ] Lead Paint Pamphlet Given to Tenant
[ ] Utilities In Tenant's Name
[ ] Keys to Tenant

DEPOSIT TO RESERVE RENTAL UNIT

Tenant/Lessee Name_____

Rental Unit Address_____

Tenant/Lessee Phone Number_____

The undersigned has hereby given a NON-REFUNDABLE deposit in the amount of _____ to reserve the rental unit listed above until _____. The Tenant/Lessee understands and agrees that this non-refundable deposit will be applied toward the first month's rent of _____ along with the security of deposit of _____ both of which are due in full on or prior to _____. If the Tenant/Lessee fails to pay first month's rent and the security deposit in full by this date, the Lessor will no longer be obligated to reserve this unit for the Tenant/Lessee; will have no obligation to rent any unit to the Tenant/Lessee; and the Tenant/Lessee will forfeit this entire deposit. In addition, if the Tenant/Lessee changes his/her mind about renting, the Tenant/Lessee will forfeit this entire deposit.

The preceding is clearly understood and agreed to by both parties.

_____   _____
Tenant/Lessee   Date

_____   _____
Lessor   Date

RENTAL APPLICATION

Neatly complete all information below. All applicants over the age of 18 must complete and sign their own application.

Applicants full name _____ Phone # _____ DOB _____

Previous Names/Maiden Name _____

Social Security # _____ Drivers License # _____ State _____ Exp. _____

Current Address _____ City _____ State _____ Zip _____

Current Landlords Name _____ Landlords Phone # _____

Current Rent _____ Rent Paid Through _____ Current Lease Expires _____

How long at this address _____ Reason for leaving _____

Previous Address _____ City _____ State _____ Zip _____

Previous Landlords Name _____ Phone # _____

How long at this address _____ Reason for leaving _____

Auto Yr _____ Make _____ Model _____ State/License Plate # _____

Present Employer _____ Position _____ Mo. Income _____

Name of Supervisor _____

Phone # _____ How long at job _____ Other income/source _____

Employers Address _____ City _____ State _____

Have you ever been evicted? [ ] Yes [ ] No   Have you ever filed for Bankruptcy? [ ] Yes [ ] No

Have you ever willfully and intentionally refused to pay any rent when due? [ ] Yes [ ] No

Name of bank _____ Branch _____ Type of Account _____

Name of bank _____ Branch _____ Type of Account _____

Personal References
Name _____ Yrs. Known _____ Relationship _____ Phone # _____

Name _____ Yrs. Known _____ Relationship _____ Phone # _____

Total number of adults _____ Total number of children living with you under the age of 18 _____

Names and relations of all other applicants _____
_____

I CERTIFY that answers given herein are true and complete to the best of my knowledge. I authorize investigation of all statements contained in this application for tenant screening and authorize the obtaining of a Consumer Credit Report, I understand that the landlord may terminate any rental agreement entered into for any misrepresentations made above.

Signature _____ Date _____

Received from applicant the non-refundable sum of $_____ dollars for tenant screening.

RESIDENTIAL LEASE

THIS AGREEMENT made and entered into on this _____ day of (mo.) _____ (yr) _____ by and between
_____ hereinafter called Lessor and
_____ hereinafter called Lessee. The
Lessor hereby leases to Lessee the premises situated in the County of _____, State of _____, Address:
_____ and consisting of
_____ upon the following TERMS and CONDITIONS:

1. TERM: The initial term hereof shall commence on (mo./day) _____, (yr) _____, and continue for a period of _____ months thereafter.
2. RENT: Rent shall be payable monthly, in advance, at a rate of _____ ($_____) per month during the term of this agreement on the first day of each calendar month to Lessor or his/her authorized agent at the following address: _____ or at other places as may be designated by Lessor from time to time. Tenant agrees to pay $25 for each dishonored check.
3. LATE FEE: Time is of the essence of this agreement. If the rent is accepted after 5pm on the 4th day of the month, a late fee of fifty dollars ($50.00) will apply to that month's rent. Any returned check will be considered as unpaid rent and will subject the Lessee to the late fee, eviction, and criminal prosecution.
4. DEFAULT AND EVICTION: If Lessee shall fail to pay rent in full by 5pm on the fourth (4th) of the month or perform any term hereof, the Lessor, at its option, upon three (3) days advance written notice to the Lessee, may terminate all rights of the Lessee hereunder; and the Lessor shall automatically and immediately have the right to take out a Dispossessory Warrant and have Lessee and his/her family and possessions evicted from the premises. If Lessee abandons or vacates the property while in said default of payment or rent, Lessor may consider any property left on premises to be abandoned and may dispose of the same in any manner allowed by law. In the event the Lessor reasonably believes that such abandoned property has no value, it may be discarded.
5. PERSONAL PROPERTY: Said lease shall include the following personal property:_____
_____.
6. UTILITIES, TAXES, AND INSURANCE: _____ shall be responsible for the payment of
_____. Lessor shall pay for any Insurance coverage for the residence structure and Lessor shall be named the beneficiary on the insurance policy and NO coverage will be provided for the Lessee or his/her family, visitors, friends, property, or liability. <u>Lessee shall obtain renter's insurance separately if Lessee desires insurance coverage.</u> Lessor shall pay all real estate taxes on the leased property.
7. PROPERTY LOSS: Lessor shall not be liable for damage to Lessee's property of any type for any reason or cause whatsoever, except where such is due to Lessor's gross negligence. Lessee acknowledges that he/she is aware that he/she is responsible for obtaining any desired insurance for fire, theft, liability, etc. on personal possessions, family, and guests.
8. USE: The premises shall be used as a residence and for no other purpose without prior written consent of Lessor.
9. ASSIGNMENT AND SUBLETTING: Lessee may not sublet residence or assign this lease without written consent of Lessor.
10. MAINTENANCE, REPAIRS, OR ALTERATIONS: Lessor shall make necessary repairs to the premises within a reasonable period of time after being notified in writing of the need for such repairs, provided that any damage caused by the carelessness of the Lessee or Lessee's guest(s) shall be repaired at the Lessee's expense. Lessee shall maintain the premises in a clean and sanitary manner and shall surrender the premises at the termination of this lease, in as good condition as received, normal wear and tear excepted. Lessee shall be responsible for damages caused by his/her negligence and that of his/her family, invitees or guests. Lessee shall maintain any surrounding grounds, including lawns and shrubbery, and keep the same clear of rubbish and weeds. Lessee shall keep lawn mowed with grass shorter than 4 inches at all times. Lessee shall be responsible to keep premises free of pest infestations (i.e. ants, roaches, mice, rats, etc.). Lessee shall not alter any portion of the premises, including painting any part of the premises, without the written consent of Lessor. If Lessor must clean-up, mow the lawn, or repair any damage caused by the Lessee, Lessee's invitees or guests, Lessee will be billed and shall pay for services performed within 15 days of the repair, cleanup, or mowing. Lessee is responsible for changing the furnace filter(s) <u>every</u> month. Lessee is responsible for the lighting of pilot light(s) if the property is equipped with a gas furnace or gas appliances. If Lessor must come to light pilot light(s), Lessee will be billed and shall pay for this service within 15 days of the lighting of the pilot light. Lessee is responsible for all glass breakage and for repairing clogged or plugged toilets, sinks, and drains. If Lessor must come to repair glass or clogged/plugged toilets, sinks, or drains, Lessee will be billed and shall pay for this service within 15 days. Failure to pay for any of these services provided by the Lessor within the 15 days shall constitute a default of this lease by the Lessee.

Page 1 of 4

© 2006 Ciara International, Inc. - All Rights Reserved Page 139 www.1minutetorentalpropertyriches.com

11. ENTRY AND INSPECTION: Lessee shall permit Lessor or Lessor's agents to enter the premises at reasonable times and upon reasonable notice for the purpose of inspecting the premises or for making necessary repairs.
12. POSSESSION: If Lessor is unable to deliver possession of the premises at the commencement hereof, Lessor shall not be liable for any damage caused thereby nor shall this agreement be void or voidable, but Lessee shall not be liable for any rent until possession is delivered. Lessee may terminate this agreement if possession is not delivered within 30 days of the commencement of the term hereof.
13. INDEMNIFICATION: Lessee releases Lessor from liability for and agrees to indemnify Lessor against losses incurred by Lessor as a result of (a) Lessee's failure to fulfill any condition of this agreement; (b) any damage or injury happening in or about residence or premises to Lessee, Lessee's family, Lessee's invitees or licensees or such person's property; (c) Lessee's failure to comply with any requirements imposed by any governmental authority; and (d) any judgement, lien, or other encumbrance filed against premises as a result of Lessee's action.
14. FAILURE OF LESSOR TO ACT: Failure of Lessor to insist upon compliance with the terms of this agreement shall not constitute a waiver of any violation.
15. REMEDIES CUMULATIVE: All remedies under this agreement or by law or equity shall be cumulative. If a suit for any breach of this agreement establishes a breach by Lessee, Lessee shall pay to Lessor all expenses incurred in connection therewith, including all attorney's fees and court costs.
16. NOTICES: Any notice required by this agreement shall be in writing and shall be delivered personally or mailed by registered or certified mail.
17. SECURITY DEPOSIT: The security deposit consideration of _____ ($_____) shall secure the performance of the Lessee's obligations hereunder. Lessor may, but shall not be obligated to, apply all or portions of said deposit on account of Lessee's obligations hereunder. Any balance remaining upon termination shall be returned to Lessee within thirty (30) days from the date possession is delivered to Lessor or Lessor's agent provided that all monies due to Lessor have been paid; all keys returned to Lessor; and premises is not damaged and is left in its original condition, normal wear and tear excepted; and management is in receipt of copy of paid final bills on all utilities and insurance. **"Normal wear and tear" shall not include such wear and tear that makes necessary the painting of the walls or woodwork more often than once every ten years, or the cleaning or repairing of the carpeting in any property more often than once every ten years, or the repairing of any holes in the ceiling, walls, or floors in any property at any time**. The Lessee shall pay to the Lessor upon demand any amount required to repair damages resulting from other than ordinary wear and tear. Deposit will not be returned if resident leaves before lease term is completed. Deposit may be applied by Lessor to satisfy all or part of Lessee's obligations and such act shall not prevent Lessor from claiming damages in excess of the deposit. Lessee may not apply the deposit to any of the rent payment.
18. TIME: Time is of the essence of this agreement.
19. RENEWAL TERM: Any holding over after expiration of the term of this lease, with the consent of the Lessor, shall be construed as a month-to-month tenancy in accordance with the terms hereof, as applicable.
20. HEIRS, SUCCESSORS: This lease shall include and insure to and bind the heirs, executors, administrators, and successors of the respective parties hereto.
21. CREDIT APPLICATION: Lessor having received and reviewed a credit application filled out by Lessee, and Lessor having relied upon the representations and statements made therein as being true and correct, has agreed to enter into this lease with Lessee. Lessee and Lessor agree the credit application the Lessee filled out when making application to lease said premises is hereby incorporated by reference and made part of this lease agreement. Lessee further agrees if he/she has falsified any statement on said application, Lessor has the right to terminate this lease agreement immediately, and further agrees that Lessor shall be entitled to keep any security deposit and any prepaid rent as liquidated damages. Lessee further agrees, in event Lessor exercises its option to terminate lease agreement, Lessee will move himself or herself, his/her family, and possessions from the premises within 24 hours of notification from Lessor of the termination of this lease agreement. Lessee further agrees to indemnify Lessor for any damages to property of Lessor including, but not limited to, the cost of making premises suitable to lease or sell to another person, and waives any right of "set off" for the security deposit and prepaid rent which was forfeited as liquidated damages.
22. FIRE AND CASUALTY; If premises becomes uninhabitable by reason of fire, explosion, or other casualty, Lessor may at its option, terminate lease agreement or repair damages within 60 days. If Lessor does not do repairs within this time or if building is fully destroyed, the lease agreement is terminated. If Lessor elects to repair damage, rent shall be abated and prorated from the date of the fire, explosion, or other casualty to the date of reoccupancy, providing that during repairs Lessee has vacated the premises and removed Lessee's possessions as required by Lessor. The date of reoccupancy shall be the date of notice that residence is ready for occupancy.

23. RULES AND REGULATIONS:
    A. SIGNS: Lessee shall not display any signs, exterior lights, or markings. No awnings or other projections or any other alterations shall be attached or added to the building without the written consent of the Lessor.
    B. LOCKS: Lessee is prohibited from adding locks to, changing, or in any way altering locks installed on the doors. All keys must be returned to Lessor of the premises upon termination of the occupancy.
    C. Entrances, walks, and driveways shall not be obstructed or used for any purpose other than ingress and egress.
    D. Radio or television aerials shall not be placed or erected on the roof or exterior without the written consent of Lessor.
    E. PARKING: Non-operative vehicles are not permitted on premises. Any such non-operative vehicle may be removed by Lessor at the expense of Lessee owning same, for storage or public private sale, at Lessor's option, and Lessee owning same shall have no right of recourse against Lessor therefor.
    F. STORAGE: No goods or materials of any kind or description which are combustible or would increase fire risk or shall in any way increase the fire insurance rate with respect to the premises or violate any law or regulation, may be taken or placed in a storage area or the residence itself. Storage in all such areas shall be at Lessee's risk and Lessor shall not be responsible for any loss or damage.
    G. WALLS: no nails, screws, or adhesive hangars except standard picture hooks, shade brackets, and curtain rod brackets may be placed in walls, cabinets, doors, woodwork, or any other part of residence.
    H. GUEST: Lessee shall be responsible and liable for the conduct of his/her guests. Act of guests in violation of the agreement or Lessor's rules and regulations may be deemed by Lessor to be a breach by Lessee. No guest may stay longer than 10 days without permission of Lessor: otherwise a $10.00 per day guest charge will be due Lessor. The following are the only people authorized under this lease to occupy the premises:
    _____
    _____
    I. NOISE: All radios, television sets, stereos, etc. must be turned down to a level of sound that does not annoy or interfere with neighbors.
    J. Resident shall maintain his/her own yard and shrubbery and furnish his/her own garbage can and trash collection service.
    K. PETS: Animals, birds, or pets of any kind shall not be permitted inside the residence at any time unless prior written approval of Lessor has been obtained.
    L. WATERBEDS: Waterbeds are not permitted on premises.
    M. ROOFS: Lessee, family, invitees, and guests are not permitted on roofs, including porch roofs at any time. Lessee shall not place or store any objects on the roof.
    N. Trampolines are not permitted on the premises.
    O. Swimming pools are not permitted on the premises.
    P. Kerosene heaters, wood burning appliances of any type, and other portable heaters are not permitted on the premises.
    Q. Grills (of any type) are not permitted to be used on covered porches, decks, or patios..
    R. Lessee agrees that the smoke detector(s) in the premises is/are under the care, custody, and control of the Lessee. The Lessee is responsible for the purchase, installation, and replacement of batteries as needed for the smoke detector(s). The Lessee agrees to test the smoke detector(s) at least twice a year. Lessee will <u>immediately</u> replace any smoke detector that is not working properly.
    S. No Illegal Activity shall be permitted on the premises. Illegal activity by Lessee, Lessee's family, or Lessee's invitees or guests shall all be deemed to be Illegal Activity by the Lessee for the purposes of this Lease and shall be cause for immediate eviction.
    T. No personal property shall be placed in common areas of multi-unit buildings. Lessee agrees that such property will be considered trash and may be disposed of AT THE LESSEE'S EXPENSE by the Lessor.
    U. Lessee will not use poison of any type, either inside or outside the residence, to deal with mice, rats, or any other pests. Traps and electronic devices are the only acceptable means of dealing with pests.
    V. Lessee shall keep utilities connected and on at all times and shall heat the premises to at least 50 degrees F at all times. Lessee shall be solely responsible for all damage caused by freezing pipes and water damage resulting from Lessee's failure to provide adequate heat. Failure to keep utilities connected and on may result in eviction.

© 2006 Ciara International, Inc. - All Rights Reserved   www.1minutetorentalpropertyriches.com

W. RESIDENT's GUIDE: Lessor reserves the right at any time to prescribe such additional rules and make such changes to the rules and regulations set forth and referred to above, as Lessor shall, in its judgement, determine to be necessary for the safety, care, and cleanliness of the premises, for the preservation of good order, or for the comfort or benefit of Lessees generally.

24. This agreement and any attached addendum constitute the entire agreement between the parties and no oral statements shall be binding. It is the intention of the parties herein that if any part of this rental agreement is invalid, for any reason, such invalidity shall not void the remainder of the agreement.

IN WITNESS HEREOF, the parties hereto have executed this agreement the day and year first above written.

For

_____   _____
          Lessee   Lessor

_____   **Send Rent Payments and Correspondence to:**
          Lessee
                                     Address_____

_____   Phone_____
          Address

RESIDENTIAL LEASE ADDENDUM TO INCLUDE CO-SIGNER

This Addendum is made this _____ day of (*mo.*)_____ (*yr.*)_____, and is added to and amends the agreement by and between _____, as Lessor, and _____, as Lessee which contract/agreement is dated the _____ day of (*mo.*)_____, (*yr.*)_____, on the following property:_____.

The undersigned person agrees to be the co-signer on the lease for _____.
The monthly rent is _____(_____) and is due in full on the 1st of each month and late after 5pm on the 4th of each month. If the rent is not received in full by 5pm on the 4th of each month, a Fifty Dollar ($50.00) late fee will be due in addition to the rent. The term of the lease is _____, beginning the _____ day of (*mo.*)_____ (*yr.*)_____ continuing until termination of the lease as outlined in the Lease. The cosigner agrees to be financially responsible for all payments not made by the Lessee on or before 5pm on the 4th of the month and agrees to pay the Lessor said payments and late fees within three (3) days of being notified by the Lessor that a payment has not been made in a timely manner. In addition, the cosigner agrees to be financially responsible for any/all damages to the Lessor's premises, building(s) and personal property caused by the Lessee and/or guest(s) of the Lessee. The cosigner agrees to pay the Lessor for any/all damages within three (3) days of being notified by the Lessor of the damages.

IN WITNESS HEREOF, the parties hereto have executed this agreement the day and year first above written.

_____   _____
            Co-signer   Lessor

_____   _____
            Co-signer   Address

_____   _____
            Address   Phone

Lease Addendum

This Addendum is made this _____ day of _____, _____, and is added to and amends the Lease dated _____, between _____, Lessor, and _____, Lessee. It is hereby agreed by all parties that _____

_____
_____
_____
_____
_____
_____.

Only the additions and amendments specifically listed above change the original lease and the Lessee hereby agrees to perform all covenants, conditions, and obligations of Lessee under the terms of the original lease dated _____, that are not specifically changed above.

_____
Lessor

_____
Date

_____
Lessee

_____
Date

Lease Addendum Allowing Pets

This Addendum is made this _____ day of _____, _____, and is added to and amends the Lease dated this _____ day of _____, _____, between _____, Lessor, and _____, Lessee. It is hereby agreed by all parties that the Lessee shall be allowed to keep _____ named _____ under the following conditions:

The Lessee shall:
1. be solely responsible for the pet and keep it quiet and under control at all times.
2. keep the pet leashed when it is outside Lessee's premises.
3. not leave the pet unattended for periods that exceed eight hours.
4. not walk the pet on any neighbor's property.
5. dispose of the pet's droppings properly and quickly.
6. keep pet from causing any annoyance or disturbance to others and will remedy immediately any complaints.
7. get rid of the pet's offspring within eight weeks of birth.
8. pay for any damage, loss, or expense caused by the pet within 15 days of being notified by the Lessor.
9. Immediately notify the Lessor of any adverse incidents involving the pet.
10. Lessor reserves the right to revoke permission to keep the pet should Lessee violate this agreement.
11. Lessee clearly understands and agrees that no dogs on the vicious dog list are permitted on the premises at any time (including during visits).
12. Lessee clearly understands and agrees that only the pet named above is permitted on the premises. The Lessee must receive WRITTEN APPROVAL from the Lessor prior to any other pets being added or substituted for the permitted pet.

_____
Lessor

_____
Date

_____
Lessee

_____
Date

© 2006 Ciara International, Inc. - All Rights Reserved   www.1minutetorentalpropertyriches.com

Lease Addendum - Property Modification Agreement

This agreement, dated _____ , is attached to and forms a part of the "Residential Lease - Rental Agreement" dated _____, between _____, Lessor, and _____, Lessee, for the residential unit located at _____.

Lessee desires to modify or make an addition to the leased property/dwelling as follows:
_____
_____
_____
_____

It is understood and agreed by both parties that the addition/modification listed above to the property/dwelling must be made in a workman like manner and that the addition/modification will be removed if the Lessor is not satisfied with the work and the premises returned to its original condition. The addition or modification made to the property/dwelling by the Lessee becomes the permanent property of the Lessor and may not be later removed or altered by the lessee. Any removal, alteration, or damage to the addition/modification will be considered damages to the Lessor and Lessee will be financially responsible for said damage.

The Lessee understands that he/she is NOT an employee of the Lessor. All modifications made by the Lessee are being made at the exclusive request of the Lessee. The Lessee is not being paid or reimbursed for his/her labor and may not deduct anything from the rent for this work.

By _____
                Lessor

By _____
                Lessee

Lease Addendum - Paint Agreement

This agreement, dated _____ , is attached to and forms a part of the Lease dated _____, between _____, Lessor, and _____, Lessee, for the residential unit located at _____.

Lessee desires to paint the following areas of the house or apartment:
_____
_____
_____
_____

It is understood and agreed by both parties that the Lessee agrees to:

1. Paint ONLY the room(s) specifically described above.
2. Lessee will repaint the room(s) specifically described above back to its original color and condition (professional quality) prior to vacating the property. Lessee agrees that an evaluation of the adequacy and quality of the repainting to the original color and condition lies solely with the Lessor. If Lessor is not satisfied with the repainting done by the Lessee or his/her painter, the Lessee agrees that Lessor may repaint the room(s) or area(s) and charge Lessee for this service. Lessee agrees to pay Lessor for this repainting within 10 days of being notified by the Lessor. At Lessor's option, this payment may be deducted from the Lessee's security deposit.
3. Lessor will add $_____ to Lessee's security deposit, any of which may be used for repainting, cleaning, repairs, or delinquent rent when Lessee vacates. This added deposit, or what remains of it when room(s) or area(s) have been repainted to the satisfaction of the Lessor, will be returned to Lessee within 30 days of vacating the property.

By _____ Lessor

By _____ Lessee

© 2006 Ciara International, Inc. - All Rights Reserved   www.1minutetorentalpropertyriches.com

MOVE-IN/MOVE-OUT FORM

Lessee's Name _____ Move In Date _____
Address _____ Move Out Date _____

MASTER BEDROOM
Walls _____
Ceiling _____
Floors _____
Door _____
Windows _____
Screens _____
Window Covering _____
Light Fixture _____

BEDROOM
Walls _____
Ceiling _____
Floors _____
Door _____
Windows _____
Screens _____
Window Covering _____
Light Fixture _____

BEDROOM
Walls _____
Ceiling _____
Floors _____
Door _____
Windows _____
Screens _____
Window Covering _____
Light Fixture _____

BEDROOM
Walls _____
Ceiling _____
Floors _____
Door _____
Windows _____
Screens _____
Window Covering _____
Light Fixture _____

BEDROOM
Walls _____
Ceiling _____
Floors _____
Door _____
Windows _____
Screens _____
Window Covering _____
Light Fixture _____

BEDROOM
Walls _____
Ceiling _____
Floors _____
Door _____
Windows _____
Screens _____
Window Covering _____
Light Fixture _____

LIVING ROOM
Walls _____
Ceiling _____
Floors _____
Door _____
Windows _____
Screens _____
Window Coverings _____
Light Fixture _____

DINING ROOM
Walls _____
Ceiling _____
Floors _____
Door _____
Windows _____
Screens _____
Window Coverings _____
Light Fixture _____

KITCHEN
Walls_____
Ceiling_____
Floors_____
Door_____
Windows_____
Screens_____
Window Coverings_____
Light Fixture_____
Sink_____
Cabinets_____
Range & Oven_____
Refrigerator_____
Dishwasher_____
Garbage Disposal_____

BATHROOM
Walls_____
Ceiling_____
Floors_____
Door_____
Windows_____
Screens_____
Window Coverings_____
Light Fixture_____
Sink_____
Medicine Cabinets_____
Commode_____
Tub/Shower_____

UTILITY ROOM
Floors_____
Walls/Ceiling_____
Washer/Dryer_____

GARAGE
Walls_____
Ceilings_____
Floor_____
Door_____
Windows_____
Screens_____
Window Coverings_____
Light Fixture_____

BATHROOM
Walls_____
Ceiling_____
Floors_____
Door_____
Windows_____
Screens_____
Window Coverings_____
Light Fixture_____
Sink_____
Medicine Cabinet_____
Commode_____
Tub/Shower_____

BATHROOM
Walls_____
Ceiling_____
Floors_____
Door_____
Windows_____
Screens_____
Window Coverings_____
Light Fixture_____
Sink_____
Medicine Cabinet_____
Commode_____
Tub/Shower_____

HVAC
Heat Source_____
Air Conditioner_____

EXTERIOR
Walls_____
Trim_____
Lawn/Landscaping_____

ITEMS GIVEN TO LESSEE
Keys_____
Garage Door Opener_____

I agree that the property is in the condition described above.

Lessee: _____ Lessee: _____

Lessor: _____

Emergency Notification Form

For

_____

Primary Contact _____

Address: _____

Relationship _____

Home Telephone _____

Cell Telephone _____

Work Telephone _____

Alternate Contact _____

Address _____

Relationship _____

Home Telephone _____

Cell Telephone _____

Work Telephone _____

Special Instructions _____

_____

_____

Disclosure of Information on Lead-Based Paint and Lead-Based Paint Hazards

Lead Warning Statement

Housing built before 1978 may contain lead-based paint. Lead from paint, paint chips, and dust can pose health hazards if not managed properly. Lead exposure is especially harmful to young children and pregnant women. Before renting pre-1978 housing, landlords must disclose the presence of known lead-based paint and/or lead-based paint hazards in the dwelling. Tenants must also receive a federally approved pamphlet on lead poisoning prevention.

Lessor's Disclosure (check as applicable)

_____(a) Presence of lead-based paint or lead-based paint hazards (check one below):

    [ ]   Known lead-based paint and/or lead-based paint hazards are present in the housing (explain).
_____
_____

    [ ]   Lessor has no knowledge of lead-based paint and/or lead-based paint hazards in the housing.

_____(b) Records and reports available to the lessor (check one below):

    [ ]   Lessor has provided the lessee with all available records and reports pertaining to lead-based paint and/or lead-based paint hazards in the housing (list documents below).
_____
_____

    [ ]   Lessor has no reports or records pertaining to lead-based paint and/or lead-based paint hazards in the housing.

Lessee's Acknowledgment (initial)
_____(c) Lessee has received copies of all information listed above.
_____(d) Lessee has received the pamphlet *Protect Your Family From Lead in Your Home*.

Certification of Accuracy

The following parties have reviewed the information above and certify, to the best of their knowledge, that the information provided by the signatory is true and accurate.

_____	_____
Lessor	Date
_____	_____
Lessee	Date
_____	_____
Lessee	Date

Rent Receipt

Date:_____

Received of _____,
$_____ for
_____(date), rent on
_____(address).

_____
Property Manager

Thank you for your business!

Paid

RENT ROLL

MONTH_____

Property	Rent/Tenant Portion	Tenant	Date Rec'd	Check/Cash
			Total	

© 2006 Ciara International, Inc. - All Rights Reserved   www.1minutetorentalpropertyriches.com

Looking for a Beautiful House or Apartment?

WE'VE GOT ONE FOR YOU!

*1, 2, & 3 Bedroom Houses & Apartments
*Many Completely Remodeled!
*We Accept Section 8!

Call Today! (xxx) xxx-xxxx

Looking for a Beautiful House or Apartment?

WE'VE GOT ONE FOR YOU!

*1, 2, & 3 Bedroom Houses & Apartments
*Many Completely Remodeled!
*We Accept Section 8!

Call Today! (xxx) xxx-xxxx

Sample Newspaper Ad:

Beautiful 1, 2, and 3 br houses and Apartments. We accept Section 8. We Love Pets!

Real Estate Funding Request

For

Joe Investor

Joe
Investor

**Real
Estate
Funding
Request**

LEAD PAINT PAMPHLET

You can download the pamphlet "Protect Your Family from Lead Paint in Your Home" at the following website: http://www.epa.gov/lead/pubs/leadpdfe.pdf

This form is required to be given to every tenant.

Intentionally Left Blank

1) Profits → come from DESPERATE Sellers

2) ALWAYS BUY at discounts or you will NOT MAKE ANY MONEY

3) NO.1 TIP → FIND Desperate Sellers and BUY AT DISCOUNT. → only way to make money in RENTALS